Triple-Play
Scrap Quilting
Planned, Coordinated, and Make-Do Styles

NANCY ALLEN

Martingale®
Create with Confidence

Dedication

To my quilting grandmothers, who both created well-loved and well-used quilts for our family.

Acknowledgments

The quilts in this book wouldn't have happened without my mother's expert binding skills. Not only did she do the binding on these 27 quilts in record time, but she has also bound just about every quilt I've made in the last 15 years. Thanks, Mom!

I must also give a big thank-you to the four terrific machine quilters who each graciously fit my quilts into their already-busy quilting schedule. Thank you to Jen Alexander (www.QuiltTopStop.com), Sue Baddley (www.SummitCreekQuilts.com), Valerie Gines (Val's Machine Quilting), and Catherine Timmons (Cat's Attic Quilting). Quilting definitely makes the quilt!

Last, but not least, thank you to the great team at Martingale. I've enjoyed every minute working with you along this journey.

Triple-Play Scrap Quilting:
Planned, Coordinated, and Make-Do Styles
© 2013 by Nancy Allen

Martingale®
19021 120th Ave. NE, Ste. 102
Bothell, WA 98011-9511 USA
ShopMartingale.com

Printed in China
18 17 16 15 14 13   8 7 6 5 4 3 2 1

Library of Congress Cataloging-in-Publication Data is available upon request.

ISBN: 978-1-60468-263-2

MISSION STATEMENT
Dedicated to providing quality products and service to inspire creativity.

CREDITS
President & CEO: Tom Wierzbicki
Editor in Chief: Mary V. Green
Design Director: Paula Schlosser
Managing Editor: Karen Costello Soltys
Acquisitions Editor: Karen M. Burns
Technical Editor: Ellen Pahl
Copy Editor: Marcy Heffernan
Production Manager: Regina Girard
Illustrator: Rose Scheifer
Cover & Text Designer: Regina Girard
Photographer: Brent Kane

Contents

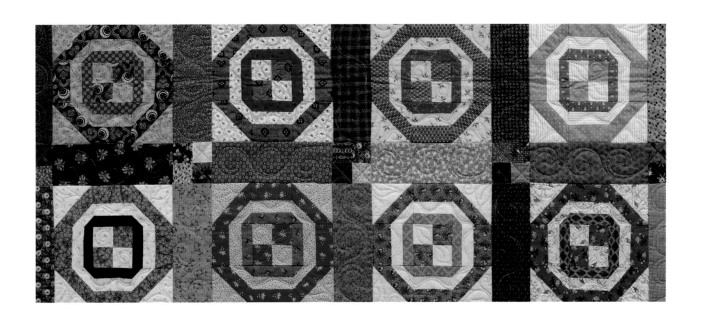

Scrap Quilts, Three Ways

If you're anything like me, your wish list of quilts gets longer with every new quilt magazine you receive; every new line of fabrics that you discover at your local quilt shop; and your own growing stash of yardage, fat quarters, and scraps. What's a girl to do? Make scrap quilts, of course!

I've written this book to encourage you to give scrap quilts a try, using any or all of my three different approaches.

MAKING DO

Making a quilt entirely from my cupboard full of scraps is so satisfying. I can be as random as I want with fabrics and colors—using as many scraps as possible, even if it's only a 2" square of a beloved fabric in a checkerboard border or a triangle from an ugly fabric that looks great when cut small and combined with lots of other fabrics. This traditional style of scrap quilt is what I call a "make-do" quilt. This is what quilters years ago did most of the time when making quilts for their beds. They made do with what they had on hand.

Since I naturally gravitate toward quilts with a traditional scrappy, make-do look, I don't throw away many scraps—the scrap cupboards in my sewing room are filled to overflowing. If you have a bulging scrap bag like I do, you'll want to consider the make-do styles in this book.

COORDINATED SCRAPS

This approach is perfect for all those fabulous precut fabrics that you fall in love with. Every week new fabrics find their way into our local quilt shops. These marvelous fabrics were designed by artists who know what quilters need to make the perfect quilt—coordinated colors; light, medium, and dark values; and large-, medium-, and small-scale prints. Choosing a collection of fabrics from one complete fabric line takes away much of the fabric and color planning—something that may be intimidating to a novice quilter—and enables you to get right to the cutting and sewing steps of your quilt, while still having a good variety of fabrics in your finished quilt.

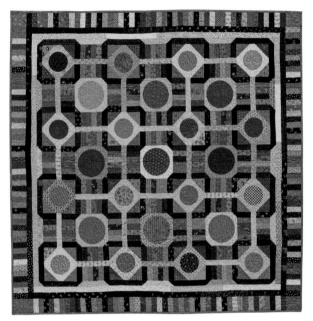

Make-do scrap version of "Just around the Corner"

Coordinated scrap version of "Just around the Corner"

I make and give many quilts as gifts, but I realize that not all of the lucky recipients prefer the traditional fabrics and make-do style that I like for myself. Creating a quilt with fabrics from a single fabric line makes it easy to find just the right combination for a quilt they'll love—whether it's a crib quilt with a cowboy theme for a new baby, or a wedding quilt for a bride-to-be who loves bold, graphic colors and patterns. Working within a single fabric line also gives me an opportunity to work out of my comfort zone of traditional fabrics. Since most fabric lines have about 40 fabrics, I still get the scrappy look I like, but it's what I call a "coordinated" scrap quilt. If you collect precuts from entire fabric lines, consider the coordinated versions of the quilts shown throughout this book.

PLANNED SCRAPPINESS

If I want a quilt to have a particular color scheme, I refer to this as a "planned" scrap quilt. Planned scrap quilts might also be from the same style of fabrics, such as homespun plaids, solid colors, or batiks—like some projects in this book. The unifying factor for each of these quilts is the color or style of fabric, but they're still scrappy and include many fabrics.

Planned scrap quilts also might involve more than one color—usually a palette of just three or four main colors, but in different values from light to dark. Examples in this book include quilts that are black, yellow, and white; pink and gray; red, aqua, and white; and red, gray, white, and black.

When you set out to make a quilt that follows a specific color scheme, such as a quilt to match the colors in your home, consider the planned quilt styles in this book, but use your own color choices.

GETTING STARTED

Each of the nine quilt designs in this book is presented three ways. The planned version uses fabrics in a limited color palette or specific style of fabrics; the coordinated version uses fabrics from the same fabric line; and the make-do version uses a wide variety of fabrics in many colors from my scrap bag and fat-quarter stash, generally not following any particular color scheme.

Specific instructions are provided for just one of the variations, but the photographs of the two other quilts will show other fabrics in addition to other ways to make the quilt different, such as varying the block size, setting the blocks with or without sashing, or using alternative borders. You'll see that it's easy to use any quilt design to make a scrappy-style quilt that is uniquely your own because of your fabric selections and simple modifications to block size and borders.

I hope you enjoy the quilts in this book and that they'll inspire you to embrace the scrappy style. Remember, the more fabrics you use, the better!

Planned scrap version of
"Just around the Corner"

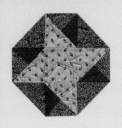

Building a Fabric Collection

Which comes first, the fabric or the quilt design? Sometimes when I begin a new project, it's because I have a collection of fabrics—scraps, precuts, or a pile of fabrics with the same color scheme—that are crying out to be cut up and sewn together into a quilt. When that's the case, I scan magazines or books in hopes of finding just the right quilt design for the fabrics. Or, I'll use quilting software to create my own design to feature the fabulous fabrics.

Other times, I may see a quilt pattern that's just my style. Then I go through my stash of fabrics to choose which ones I want to use for the design. I'll mix and match fabrics, consider their value and the scale of the pattern, and figure out whether I have enough fabric for the desired quilt. I love to "shop" from my fabric stash and make quilts from the fabrics I've gathered over the years.

But what if you don't have a big stash of fabrics, or you have a new color scheme in mind? After years of experience with collecting fabrics—after all, collecting fabric *is* a different hobby from making quilts— I've built a large stash and developed some personal guidelines for buying fabric so that I'll have enough for a quilt even if I don't yet know what that quilt will be.

Review this section to help you decide which fabrics to buy—and how much—even when you don't yet have a specific quilt in mind. Just remember that fabrics are only available for a short time. If you don't buy them when you see them, they may be gone the next time you visit the shop.

BUYING FABRICS FOR A SPECIFIC QUILT

If left to my own devices, I'll come home from the fabric shop with lots of medium-value fabrics, but only a few light and dark fabrics. For quilts to really "sing," they need light, medium, and dark fabrics. To show off the detailed piecing that goes into a block, you usually don't want the fabrics to blend together. You don't want light fabrics next to other lights, or medium fabrics next to other mediums. It takes contrast among the fabrics in your block to highlight the block's pattern.

Remove the Color
Use photo-editing software to convert a color photo to black and white. It's easier to see the value of the fabrics. Colors, especially yellow, can be misleading when identifying value. The top fabric in the medium stack shown in the photo is probably more of a medium dark and needs to be moved to the dark stack.

Fabrics sorted into light, medium, and dark piles

Values are easier to see in black and white.

Of course, you can buy one of the many incredible quilt kits assembled by creative quilters at your local quilt shop. You can find block-of-the-month programs all over the Internet. And sometimes the quilt design and fabric selection in a kit or block of the month will really speak to you. If so, go for it and enjoy the process of making a quilt in which many of the fabric and design decisions have already been made. Blocks of the month and kits are often a great way to achieve a scrappy look if your stash is still growing or if you need to break out of your fabric comfort zone to make a quilt with fabrics in styles and colors that you don't have in your stash.

For example, my first foray into working with 1930s prints was through a block-of-the-month program. By the time the 12 months were up, I had a finished 1930s-style quilt as well as some great scraps and some newly acquired fat quarters to make my next 1930s-style quilt.

Reproduction 1930s prints ready for a planned scrap quilt

BUYING FABRICS FOR A MAKE-DO SCRAP QUILT

For make-do scrap quilts, I buy mostly fat quarters. If the quilt shop doesn't have precut fat quarters, I'll buy ⅓-yard cuts (12" x 42"). I've found that the standard ¼-yard cut (9" x 42") doesn't give me enough flexibility for cutting the fabric into different-sized pieces, and ½ yard is probably more than I need. If I absolutely love a fabric, I'll buy a whole yard.

When I find a fabric that will be a great background in a quilt or a repeated light value in blocks, I typically buy two or three yards. If I don't use it all in one quilt, I may have enough left over for a wall quilt, or it will be used as light scraps in other quilts. Although I often use multiple background fabrics to give a scrappier look to my make-do quilts, using a common background fabric helps to unify random fabrics from my scrap bag. Using one background fabric also means I can focus most of my time on selecting dark and medium scraps. I don't have to search for a background as well. Similarly, if I see a fabric that I may want to use as a primary focus in the quilt, either for a border or to be repeated in each block, I'll buy at least one yard, more if the fabric has a large motif and I may want to use it as a border. That will allow me to cut it lengthwise without obvious piecing.

I also buy yardage—usually one yard—of the occasional medium or dark fabric that reads as a solid from a distance. These fabrics are usually tone-on-tone fabrics, or they have a small neutral pattern on the dark background. They're great unifiers in a scrap quilt because when repeated in the quilt, such as in an alternate block, or in sashing, or a border, they give your eye a place to rest before jumping to one of the scrappy blocks in the quilt, thereby "grounding" the quilt.

I'll often use a particular fabric in multiple make-do quilts. Since I like to use a lot of different fabrics in a quilt, I may use only a few strips from a fat quarter in any one particular quilt. I then keep those partially used fat quarters together and look there when I need another strip or a few squares of fabric for a different quilt. Eventually all that remains from the fat quarter are miscellaneous strips and squares, at which point those pieces go into the scrap pile for when I need lesser quantities of a given fabric. The fabric will eventually all be used!

BUYING FABRICS FOR A COORDINATED QUILT

If you love the many fabric lines released each month—and who doesn't?—precuts are a great way to quickly assemble fabrics for a coordinated scrap quilt. But how much of the fabric line should you buy? I typically begin with a precut pack of 10" squares, which is about the equivalent of 2½ yards of fabric or 10 fat quarters. I like 10" squares, because they can easily be cut into four 5" charm squares, five 2"-wide strips, or four 2½"-wide strips. By buying 10"-square precuts, I also know that I have 40 coordinated fabrics to mix and match in my quilt for that scrappy look and feel. I will often add a precut roll of 2½"-wide strips to the mix for a scrappy sashing or border.

I also pick out three or four fabrics from the collection and buy some yardage—usually one fabric in a light value, one or two in a medium value, and one in a dark value. For example, I might buy two yards of the light value to use as a background, one yard of the medium to use as a border, and ½ yard of the dark to use as a contrasting binding or sashing.

Sometimes my precut acquisitions are impulse purchases at my local quilt shop. They then sit in my sewing room for a couple months (or longer!) looking pretty before I get around to using them. Unfortunately, by then my local quilt shop has run out of the accompanying yardage. This is where Internet search engines can save the day—and may save you some money at the same time. By the time a line of fabric has been out in the marketplace for a few months, many online shops put what is left in their inventory on sale.

I try not to get too attached to any one fabric, because it may no longer be available, but I'll determine how much additional light, medium, and dark fabric I need and begin my online search. I usually begin with Quiltshops.com and search using the name of the fabric line. Within just a few seconds, various quilt shops will show which fabrics in the line are still available. I find the shop that has the best selection at the lowest price and buy just what I need to complete the quilt. Since I try to centralize all of my purchases with one shop, shipping is usually only about $5. But the savings is often $2 or more per yard compared to when the fabric was first released. Who doesn't want to save some money on fabric?

Coordinated fabrics from the same fabric line in a variety of yardages, values, and print scales

Precuts and yardage of coordinated fabrics from two different fabric lines

BUYING FABRICS FOR A PLANNED QUILT

Collecting fabric for a planned quilt isn't difficult, but it will take longer than simply buying a single fabric line. However, the hunt is part of the fun! When I go on the annual quilt-shop hop in my area, I usually have a couple of planned quilts in mind as I visit each shop. This past spring, I was able to find many of the black, yellow, and white prints I used in the planned version of "Just around the Corner" (page 22) as well as homespun plaids for the planned "Plaza Mayor" (page 34). Not only was I gathering fabrics for these specific quilts and supporting my local quilt shops, but I also avoided buying a lot of random fabrics (at least, not too many).

Homespun plaids featured in "Plaza Mayor"

Black, yellow, and white prints from "Just around the Corner"

Before beginning a planned quilt, I first decide on the color scheme for the quilt. A single fabric that I love, or the colors in a photograph might inspire the color scheme. Or I may simply want to play with some of the fabrics in my stash. Once in a while a fabric company releases a line of fabric that uses a limited palette, and it becomes the starting point for a planned quilt. Since fabric lines typically come in multiple colorways, one of the colorways may fit with the chosen color scheme.

There are new color trends each year; it might be easy to find certain colors across multiple fabric lines one year, but they may not be as common the next year. For example, it has been easy to find red, white, and aqua fabrics over the past year because the color combination has been very popular in multiple fabric lines. I even found a couple great aqua and white options from a line of aqua, lime-green, and white prints because some of the fabrics used only aqua and white and no green. Keep your eyes peeled, and you'll find plenty of fabrics that will all work together.

When I set out to make the red, white, and aqua planned version of "Days of '47" (page 52), I could have bought only a few fabrics and then repeated each fabric in each block in the quilt. But I think the quilt is much more interesting because it has a dozen or more fabrics that adhere to the planned color scheme throughout the blocks. Some of the fabrics are red tone on tone; some are aqua tone on tone; and some are red, aqua, and white. I also looked for some variation in the scale of the print and made sure to get fabrics in a variety of light, medium, and dark values. When they were all put together into blocks, sashing, and borders, the result was a limited color palette, but the quilt still has that homey, scrappy feel.

Red, aqua, and white color scheme for planned quilt

When making a planned quilt, I typically buy fat quarters or ⅓-yard cuts complemented by some yardage in light, medium, and dark values, much like I do for make-do and coordinated quilts.

I've also been able to find collections of 10" squares based on different color schemes. These collections were a great starting point for some of my quilts with a planned color scheme. You do have to be careful when shopping online, because the colors can look different on your computer screen than in real life, but I've only had a couple color surprises when the fabrics arrived.

Look for the Edge

If you want to remember the name of the fabric line a particular fat quarter comes from, check to make sure that the fat quarter includes the printed selvage with the name of the line. When selecting the fat quarters at a shop, I unfold them to find one that includes this. Then, if I need more of that fabric later, I can do a quick search online to find additional yardage. (Be sure to refold any fat quarters carefully and place them neatly back on the shelf if they don't have the printed selvage.)

Printed selvage edges serve as a reminder of the fabric line.

Planning a Scrap Quilt

My philosophy is that any quilt design can be turned into a planned, coordinated, or make-do scrap quilt—even quilts that were originally designed with a total of only four or five fabrics. But how do you look at a quilt that has only a few fabrics and give it a scrappy style? What if you love a quilt pattern and want it with different fabrics or colors than the original design? Or perhaps you just don't want the same quilt, with the same fabrics dozens of other quilters are using. What if you want to put your own spin on the fabric selection or make the quilt a different size than the original? Read through this section of the book to get answers to these questions and information that will help you plan your quilt and gather the fabrics. You'll gain confidence in your ability to look at a pattern and know how to make the quilt uniquely your own.

PLANNED, COORDINATED, OR MAKE-DO

First decide what style of scrap quilt you want to make. If you want a quilt that matches a particular color scheme, such as that in a baby's nursery, perhaps a planned scrap quilt is the right option for you. If you have some precuts from a favorite line of fabrics, then choose the coordinated option. If you have a growing stash of fat quarters and scraps left over from other quilts, then why not try a make-do scrap quilt.

COLOR SCHEME

Your first decision is about color. For a coordinated quilt using a single fabric line, the color decisions have been made for you, although it was most likely the colors in the line that first drew you to it.

If you're making a planned scrap quilt, decide what color scheme you're going to use. Typically you'll pick one to three colors and add a neutral that works with them.

Although make-do scrap quilts don't necessarily follow a color scheme, you may want a particular color or two to be prevalent in the quilt. Be sure to select several fabrics in that color, scatter them throughout your quilt, and consider using them in the borders or sashing.

BACKGROUND FABRIC

The background fabric combines with the other fabrics in the block to help create the main block design. Although a light background fabric is the popular choice, background fabrics can also be medium or dark values. Don't be afraid of prints that will give added dimension and interest to the quilt.

This block in the make-do version of "Days of '47" has a light background.

The blocks from the coordinated version of "A Star is Born" all have medium-value background fabrics.

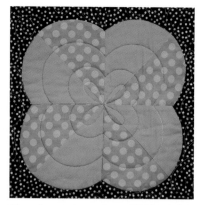

The planned version of "Cherish Is the Word" features a dark background.

Do you want to use the same background fabric throughout the quilt, as I did with the make-do "Best Friends Forever" quilt? Using the same background fabric is a good choice if you're just getting started with scrappy style, have a great background fabric in your stash, or simply want to help unify your other fabric selections.

To go a bit scrappier, use a different background fabric for each block in the quilt, like I did in the make-do "Days of '47" quilt (page 53). You can also use multiple background fabrics in the same block for a scrappier look. Review the block illustrations below to see how the changes increase the scrappiness of each block.

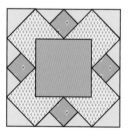

Same light
background print

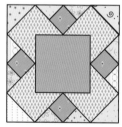

Assorted light
background prints

Assorted medium-value
background prints

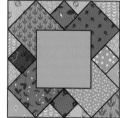

Assorted
medium-value prints

You may choose not to include what is typically considered a background fabric. In the examples below, I simply combined fabrics that I thought looked great together. I relied on color, value, and print scale to provide the contrast between pieces in the blocks.

*Block from coordinated
"Bricks and Cobblestones" quilt*

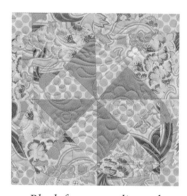

*Block from coordinated
"Cherish Is the Word" quilt*

In the block shown below, I used both light and dark background fabrics in opposite corners and repeated those fabrics in all of the blocks. If you look at the final coordinated "Bull's Eye" quilt on page 71, you'll see that a secondary hourglass pattern appears where the blocks come together.

Block from coordinated "Bull's Eye" quilt

VALUE AND CONTRAST

Value has to do with how light or dark a fabric is. When fabrics with the same value are placed next to each other, there is little contrast, and your eye tends to blend the fabrics. Sometimes that's the effect that you want, as in the coordinated "Cherish Is the Word" (page 65).

Traditionally, however, quilts have noticeable contrast among the fabrics in order to highlight a block's piecing or appliqué design. As you vary which parts of the block are light, medium, or dark, the block takes on a completely different look. Consider the variations below of a Variable Star block and the Salt Lake City block used in the "Days of '47" quilt (page 48). You might want to use the same value placement in each block throughout your quilt, or mix it up for more variety.

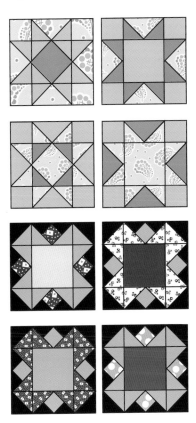

Of course, the lightest fabric you can have in a quilt is white and the darkest is black. My planned "Just around the Corner" quilt in yellow, black, and white (page 22) takes advantage of this contrast to create the secondary white pattern that links the smaller appliquéd circles and black solid that frames the blocks.

Perhaps you want a quilt that has an overall dark, or low-key, appearance. Although my make-do "Bricks and Cobblestones" (page 47) uses some light fabrics to create the cobblestones at the center of the blocks and for the border, the quilt uses mostly medium and dark fabrics. As a result, the quilt reads as a dark quilt.

Value is also a consideration in the overall quilt setting. For example, each of the blocks in my planned "Plaid and Pinwheels" (page 78) uses only three fabrics. I made sure to use only light- and medium-value fabrics for the blocks and sashing. However, I incorporated darker grays (almost black) into the pinwheel and checkerboard borders, thereby framing the center block area and highlighting the detailed piecing that went into the borders.

I relied on higher contrast for the "Just around the Corner" quilts (pages 22, 28, and 29). The use of black and white—both in the blocks and in the first pieced border—creates one of the secondary patterns in the planned version of the quilt. Using medium-dark-blue fabrics in combination with light fabrics creates this design in the coordinated version. And using blacks and tans does the same in the make-do version.

Planned quilt uses black and white for contrast.

Coordinated quilt contrast comes from light and medium-dark-blue fabrics.

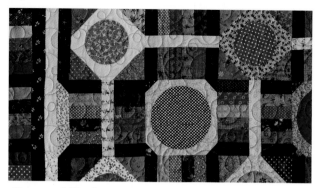

Tans and blacks create contrast in the make-do quilt.

From coordinated "Plaza Mayor"

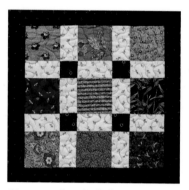

From make-do "Plaza Mayor"

SASHING

Depending on your fabric choices, sashing can be a major design element in the quilt, or it can simply set the blocks apart. For example, my planned "Days of '47" quilt in red, aqua, and white (page 52) has pieced sashing that is essential to the quilt's design. It helps to create the alternate nine-patch design between the blocks. Similarly, the pieced sashing for the planned and coordinated versions of "Plaza Mayor" (pages 34 and 35) ties into the block's grid design. However, for the make-do version, I chose a plain sashing without cornerstones to simply frame the blocks. In each of these four quilts, I used the same fabrics throughout the quilt for the sashing strips, whether they were pieced or not.

Your sashing doesn't have to be made from the same fabrics throughout the quilt as in the above examples. The sashing for the make-do "Bull's Eye" quilt (page 66) uses many different fabrics and it's still a key design element that adds to the make-do style.

PULLING IT ALL TOGETHER

After you've selected fabrics for your quilt, it's time to think about each block individually. How many fabrics will be in each block? For a planned or coordinated quilt, chances are good that you will use only three or four fabrics in each block, depending on the complexity of the block. Select the fabrics for each block so that there is sufficient variety in color, value, and scale of print to show off the block's design.

When creating make-do scrap quilts, don't be concerned about making each block match the others. Instead, focus your fabric selection on creating individual blocks using fabrics that "go together." As long as individual blocks are pleasing to the eye, they'll look good with the other blocks in the quilt. Your sashing and border fabrics will tie the blocks together, as will a common background fabric if you choose to use one.

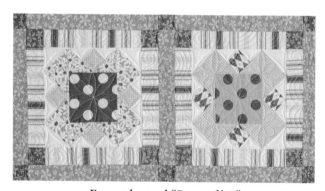

From planned "Days of '47"

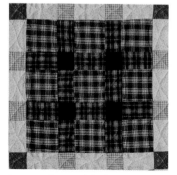

From planned "Plaza Mayor"

Making the Basic Blocks

Many of the blocks in this book are made from simple units that I call "basic blocks." Once you've perfected these basic blocks, you can put them together in thousands of ways. In most cases, there are several alternative methods for making the blocks. These are my favorites, but experiment with different techniques to find your own preferred methods.

Before You Begin

Here are a few notes about assumptions in the project instructions.

- Yardage amounts and cutting instructions are based on 42"-wide usable fabric after you've trimmed your selvages. I like to trim selvages before cutting fabrics.
- If fat quarters are indicated, they should measure at least 18" x 21". Fat eighths should measure at least 9" x 21".
- Rotary-cutting measurements include a ¼" seam allowance.
- All strips from yardage are cut across the width of fabric (selvage to selvage) unless otherwise indicated. If cutting strips from fat quarters or fat eighths, cut them along the 21" length.
- Binding strips are cut 2¼" wide, but yardage allows for strips to be cut 2½" wide if desired.
- Patterns for appliqué templates do not include seam allowances.

MAKING TWO- AND FOUR-PATCH UNITS

The two- and four-patch units are the simplest of the basic blocks and are easiest to sew. You'll find them in many quilt blocks and quilt designs. I've used four-patch units in blocks, borders, and as sashing cornerstones in various designs in this book. Start with individual squares if you want scrappy two- and four-patch units; use the second method (strip piecing) if you want several units using the same fabrics.

Method 1: Squares

1. Begin with four squares cut to the same size, as indicated in the quilt instructions. Squares are cut ½" larger than the finished size. Depending on the quilt design, the four-patch unit may have two pairs of matching fabrics, or the lights and darks will be different for a scrappier look.

2. Match two contrasting fabric squares right sides together and sew along one side. Press the seam allowances toward the darker fabric. Repeat to make two two-patch units.

3. Join the two-patch units with contrasting fabrics next to each other, matching and pinning the opposing seams before sewing. Press the seam allowances in one direction or spin the seam allowances as described on page 16.

Method 2: Strips

1. Cut two strips to the width indicated in the quilt instructions. If the instructions give the size for cutting squares, this is also the width to cut strips. Place the two strips right sides together and sew along the length of the strips. Press the seam allowances toward the darker fabric.

2. Crosscut the strip set into two-patch units, each measuring the same width as the original strips.

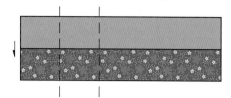

3. Join two two-patch units with contrasting fabrics next to each other, matching and pinning the opposing seams before sewing. Press the seam allowances in one direction or spin the seam allowances as described below.

Spinning the Seam Allowances

This technique minimizes bulk where the two-patch units are sewn together. It also makes it easier to sew together multiple four-patch units because the seam allowances will naturally oppose each other.

1. Before pressing the four-patch unit, use a seam ripper to remove a couple stitches from the seam allowance above the center seam.

Remove stitching
above crossed seams.

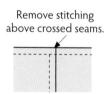

2. Position your thumbs on the horizontal seam joining your two-patch units. Gently push the left seam allowances up and pull the right seam allowances down. If you pressed the two-patch seam allowances toward the darker fabric, you will be finger-pressing the remaining seam allowances toward the lighter fabrics. Where all of the seams come together, you will see a mini four-patch design after spinning the seam allowances. You can now press the four-patch unit.

Two-Patch Tip

When sewing two-patch units into four-patch units, I suggest that you get into the habit of always orienting your two-patch units so that the seam allowances on the underneath unit are pressed toward you and the seam allowances on the top unit are pressed away from you. If you pressed the two-patch seam allowances toward the darker fabric, this will mean the top two-patch unit will have the darker fabric at the top. This ensures the seams nest together and the underneath seam allowances won't inadvertently flip up when they cross over your sewing machine's feed dogs. It also means that all of the seam allowances for your four-patch units will spin in the same direction—clockwise in this case. When making a checkerboard border where light and dark values of fabric alternate, it will be easier to assemble the border if all of the seam allowances spin in the same direction.

MAKING HALF-SQUARE-TRIANGLE UNITS

I use different sewing-machine feet for making half-square-triangle units, depending on the method I've chosen. When making them from squares, I use a ¼" patchwork foot. It makes it easy to sew ¼" away from the drawn line. When making half-square-triangle units from cut triangles, I use a ¼" patchwork foot with a built-in fabric guide. And when making the half-square-triangle units using triangle paper foundations, I use an open-toe foot (often used for machine appliqué) so I can more easily see the sewing lines. Check with your machine dealer to see which of these options are available for your sewing-machine model.

Starting with Squares

When I need only a few half-square-triangle units, this is my preferred method of making them.

1. Cut squares the size given in the quilt instructions (usually ⅞" larger than the desired finished size). Draw a diagonal line from corner to corner on the wrong side of the lighter fabric. This will be the cutting line. Stitch a scant ¼" seam allowance from each side of the marked diagonal line.

2. Cut on the drawn line and press the seam allowances toward the darker triangle. Each pair of squares yields two matching half-square-triangle units.

Cut Oversize

If you like to cut oversize and trim after sewing as I do, round up the size of the squares to the next full or half-inch increment—cutting the squares ⅛" larger than the quilt instructions. After sewing and pressing, square up the blocks using a square ruler.

Using Specialty Rulers

There are many specialty rulers on the market for cutting half-square triangles. These rulers enable you to cut triangles from strips the same width as the unfinished half-square-triangle unit. For example, if you want 2½" half-square-triangle units that will finish at 2", simply begin with 2½"-wide fabric strips. I choose this method of making half-square-triangle units when the quilt already uses fabric strips—precut or otherwise. There is also very little fabric waste since corners aren't cut away as with the method using squares. Follow the manufacturer's instructions for using the ruler.

Using Triangle Papers

I like to use triangle paper foundations when I'm making smaller half-square-triangle units, such as those that finish 2", 1½", or smaller. Purchase triangle paper foundations in a variety of sizes, or find printable files online and print your own.

Although you can use triangle paper foundations to mass-produce half-square-triangle units from fabric strips or squares with continuous sewing, I also use triangle paper foundations when I'm making lots of half-square-triangle units from miscellaneous fabric scraps. There's no need to precut the fabric to size because that will be done after sewing. The result is a pair of matching half-square-triangle units. *Note:* The instructions that accompany your triangle paper foundations will show you how to make multiple matching half-square-triangle units at a time. These instructions are for making a pair of half-square-triangle units from scraps.

To make a pair of half-square-triangle units from scraps, simply cut the triangle paper into individual rectangles along the marked cutting lines. Layer two fabric scraps that are slightly larger than the trimmed triangle paper with right sides together and the light fabric on top. Place the triangle paper foundation on top of the fabrics and stitch on the diagonal sewing lines. Cut apart the triangles and trim even with the edges of the triangle paper. Press toward the darker triangle, and then remove the triangle paper foundation.

MAKING PINWHEEL UNITS

1. Make four half-square-triangle units using one of the above methods.

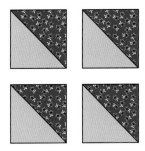

2. Lay out the half-square-triangle units as shown on page 18 and sew two half-square-triangle units together. The bias seams in the two half-square-triangle units should nest with each other, making it easy to line up the seams. Press the

seam allowances in the same direction (generally toward the darker fabric).

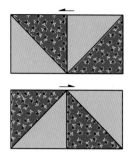

3. Place the units from step 2 right sides together so that the intersections of the seams are lined up. I typically place a pin from the intersection on the top unit down through the intersection of the bottom unit, and then place pins on each side to hold it together. Sew the rows together to finish the block. Spin the seam allowance as described on page 16.

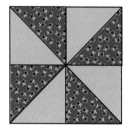

Baste First

Until you perfect your pinning and sewing technique, I suggest that you baste across the intersection of the two seams. Simply select a longer stitch length and sew an inch before the seam and an inch after. Open up the block to make sure everything is aligned. If it looks good, return your stitch length to normal and sew the entire length of the seam.

MAKING FLYING-GEESE UNITS

There are many ways to make flying-geese units, but these are the methods I use most often.

Method 1: Squares and Rectangles

1. Cut two squares and one rectangle to the sizes given in the quilt instructions. Draw a diagonal line from corner to corner on the wrong side of the squares; this will be your sewing line. Place a marked square on one end of the rectangle, right sides together. Sew on the line and trim seam allowances to ¼". Press the seam allowances toward the corner.

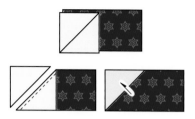

2. Place another marked square on the opposite end of the rectangle, orienting the diagonal in the opposite direction from the first piece. Stitch on the diagonal line, trim seam allowances to ¼", and press the seam allowances toward the corner.

Method 2: Triangles

This method makes four matching flying-geese units, which is what you need for making Variable Star blocks.

1. Cut one square to the size given in the quilt instructions. This size should be the finished width of the flying-geese unit plus 1¼". Cut the square into quarters diagonally; these triangles will be the center of the flying-geese units.

2. Cut four squares to the size given in the quilt instructions. The squares are usually the height of the finished flying-geese unit plus ⅞". Cut the squares in half diagonally to yield eight half-square triangles; these triangles will be the sides of the flying-geese units.

3. Sew a side triangle to the short side of a quarter-square triangle using a ¼" seam allowance. Press the seam allowances toward the side triangle. Repeat on the other side. Repeat with the other triangles to make three more flying-geese units.

Handy Rulers

I like to use one of the many specialty rulers readily available to cut the half-square and quarter-square triangles from strips. When you use these rulers to cut the triangles, you'll be trimming the triangle points. This makes it easy to align the triangles for precision piecing.

MAKING HOURGLASS UNITS

Hourglass units are also known as quarter-square-triangle units. Of course you can cut four quarter-square triangles and sew them together, but the method below enables you to make two matching hourglass units from two fabric squares. If you want scrappier units, use a variety of fabric squares for step 1. Then mix and match the results from step 2 to make hourglass units that have four fabrics in them.

1. Cut two fabric squares as indicated in the quilt instructions. I like to square up my finished units, so I cut the squares ¼" larger than the actual size needed (1¼" plus ¼", or 1½" larger than the finished size of the hourglass unit). Each pair of fabrics will make two hourglass units.

2. Draw a diagonal line from corner to corner on the wrong side of the lighter fabric square. Layer the marked square right sides together with the other fabric square and align all of the raw edges. Stitch ¼" from each side of the marked diagonal line. Carefully cut the square in half along the marked line. Press the seam allowances toward the darker fabric. *Note:* You have just made two half-square-triangle units from squares.

3. On the wrong side of one of the half-square-triangle units from step 2, draw a diagonal line from corner to corner across the seam. Place the two half-square-triangle units right sides together, making sure the top fabrics are facing the opposite fabrics underneath. Nest the seams against each other and pin to secure.

4. Stitch a scant ¼" seam allowance on each side of the marked diagonal line. Carefully cut the square in half along the marked line. You'll have two matching hourglass units. Spin the seam allowances as shown on page 16, or press the seam allowances in one direction.

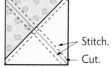 Stitch. Cut.

5. Square up the hourglass units to the size needed. Use a square ruler with a 45° diagonal line and align the diagonal line with a diagonal seam on the hourglass unit. Determine the center measurement of the hourglass block by dividing the overall block dimensions by two. For example, if you will be trimming the block to 4½" x 4½", the center of the block will be 2¼". Align the center of the block with the center measurement on the ruler. Trim away any excess from the top and right sides of the unit. Rotate the hourglass unit 180°. Align the newly cut edges with the 4½" lines of your ruler and trim the remaining sides.

2¼"

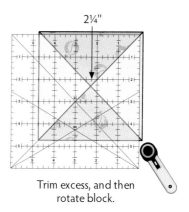

Trim excess, and then rotate block.

My favorite part of the quiltmaking process is picking out fabrics, and then combining them into blocks. By the time the quilt top is finished, I'm ready to play with some new fabric and move on to another quilt. Therefore, I choose to have my quilt tops quilted by one of the fabulous machine quilters in my area.

Not every quilt is destined to become an heirloom. Since I give quilts to family members when they get married or have babies—and I'm perfectly happy seeing those quilts get used—I need to find budget alternatives for quilts that will be well loved and well used.

BUDGET OPTION: OVERALL MEANDERING DESIGN

Usually the cheapest option for quilting is an overall meandering or stippling design. Most machine quilters have perfected this free-motion technique, and it's a great option for scrappy quilts. I often opt for a simple meandering design for a quilt that has a complex design. The meandering will complement the quilt, but the quilt design will predominate. I selected a meandering design for several quilts in this book.

A meandering design was used in the coordinated "Best Friends Forever."

MIDPRICED OPTION: DIGITIZED EDGE-TO-EDGE DESIGN

For a midpriced quilting option, search out a quilter who has a computerized long-arm machine and a good selection of digitized designs. This gives you more options for an allover quilting design. You can select a design that coordinates with the fabrics in the quilt or the quilt design, or choose it simply because you like it.

The make-do "Best Friends Forever" is quilted with a star design to complement the Star blocks and the neutral star-print backing fabric.

The allover Baptist Fan quilting design gives the coordinated "A Star Is Born" quilt a traditional look and feel.

Mix and Match

Some machine quilters will do a semi-custom quilt design by using an overall motif for the quilt center but a custom design in the borders. This gives you an original look at a lower price than a completely custom-quilted quilt.

PRICIEST OPTION: CUSTOM QUILTING

All quilts would look great with a custom quilting design. However, since this is the priciest option for machine quilting, I reserve this for quilt designs that will really benefit from the unique, one-of-a-kind quilting and for those quilts that I expect will become family heirlooms.

Custom quilting in the planned
"Just around the Corner"

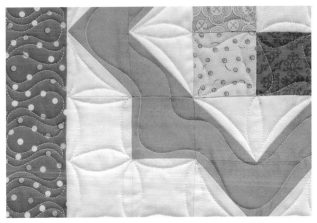

Custom quilting in make-do "A Star Is Born"

BINDING

I like a narrow binding to finish my quilts. Therefore, I cut my binding strips, which are folded in half before they're sewn to the quilt, 2¼" wide. I then use either a full-size sewing-machine foot or a walking foot—rather than a ¼" foot—while attaching the binding, so that I'm taking full advantage of the machine's feed dogs.

It's important that the binding is completely filled with the quilt sandwich when you sew it down to the back of the quilt and that there is no slack in the fabric, because that will cause your binding to more quickly wear out. If you prefer to cut your binding strips 2½" wide for a slightly wider binding, use a ⅜" seam allowance when sewing the binding to the quilt. I also use 2½" strips for binding flannel quilts, but I use a ¼" seam allowance to allow sufficient fabric to wrap around the bulkier quilt sandwich created by the flannel.

There's More Online

For more information on quiltmaking basics, visit ShopMartingale.com/HowtoQuilt. You'll find free, detailed instructions for rotary cutting your fabrics, strip piecing, chain piecing, paper piecing, appliqué, and finishing your quilt.

Just around the Corner

Pieced by Nancy Allen; custom machine quilted by Jen Alexander

Finished quilt: 73½" x 91½" • Finished block: 9" x 9"

This is the perfect quilt to use strip-piecing techniques, as well as to hone your appliqué skills. It has three blocks: a large-circle appliqué block, a small-circle appliqué block, and an alternate pieced block. The pieced inner border really enhances the design, giving the illusion of being part of the small-circle appliqué blocks.

The Planned Quilt

I'd been collecting fabrics for a black, white, and yellow quilt for a while, and had amassed a stash of fat quarters and 10" squares, not to mention yardage of solid black and white. As this design evolved, I played with the placement of the black and white solids, and was thrilled with the secondary pattern they formed. What's more, the appliquéd circles really highlight the bold, graphic fabrics I had collected. Since this planned variation has so much visual impact, I opted to keep the border design very simple—just narrow white and black borders.

MATERIALS

Yardage is based on 42"-wide fabric unless otherwise noted.

3⅔ yards of white solid for blocks, inner pieced border, and middle border (this must be the lightest light fabric in the quilt)

3½ yards *total* of assorted black, yellow, and black-and-white prints for appliqué and alternate blocks*

2⅜ yards of black solid for alternate blocks, pieced inner border, and outer border (this must be the darkest dark fabric in the quilt)

1¼ yards of yellow-and-white print for small-circle appliqué blocks

¾ yard of fabric for binding

5⅝ yards of fabric for backing

82" x 100" piece of batting

Note: I used different fabrics for each of the circle appliqués—a total of 32 different fabrics. For each of the 12 large-circle appliqués, you'll need at least a 9" square. For each of the small-circle appliqués, you will need at least a 7" square. The rest of the fabrics can be a variety of traditional ¼-yard cuts (or fat quarters).

CUTTING

Refer to "Making the Blocks" on page 24 before cutting the circle appliqués.

From the assorted black, yellow, and black-and-white prints, cut:
12 A circles
20 B circles
64 strips, 2" x 21"

From the black solid, cut:
26 strips, 2" x 42"; crosscut *16 strips* in half. Crosscut the 10 remaining strips into:
  14 rectangles, 2" x 9½"
  4 rectangles, 2" x 11"
  76 squares, 2" x 2"
9 strips, 2½" x 42"

From the white solid, cut:
20 strips, 2" x 42"; crosscut *12 strips* into:
  45 rectangles, 2" x 9½"
  4 squares, 2" x 2"
8 strips, 9½" x 42"; crosscut into 32 squares, 9½" x 9½"

From the yellow-and-white print, cut:
9 strips, 4¼" x 42"; crosscut into 80 squares, 4¼" x 4¼"

From the binding fabric, cut:
9 strips, 2¼" x 42"

Fabric Tip

For my quilt, I was able to purchase two packs of 10" squares, each with 25 yellow, black, and white prints. I supplemented this with six traditional ¼-yard cuts of additional yellow, black, and white prints. From one pack of 25 squares I had enough fabric for all but seven of my circle appliqués, and from the other pack of 25 squares (cut into 2" x 10" strips), I had enough fabric (along with the black solid) to strip piece my alternate blocks.

MAKING THE BLOCKS

The quilt has 12 A large-circle appliqué blocks, 20 B small-circle appliqué blocks, and 31 pieced blocks. The patterns for the circle appliqués are on page 27.

Pieced Blocks

1. Mix and match the various black, yellow, and black-and-white 2" x 21" strips and sew four strips together lengthwise. Add a black 2" x 21" strip to each long side to make a strip set that is 9½" x 21". Press all of the seam allowances in the same direction, being careful to keep the seams pressed flat and even. Crosscut into 4½"-wide segments. Repeat until you have 62 segments.

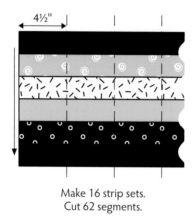

Make 16 strip sets.
Cut 62 segments.

2. Sew a white 2" x 9½" strip between two segments from step 1. Press the seam allowances toward the white strip. Repeat to make a total of 31 units.

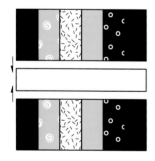 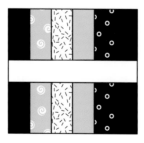

Make 31.

Appliquéd Blocks

If you need more information on how to appliqué, visit ShopMartingale.com/HowtoQuilt.

1. Draw a diagonal line from corner to corner on the wrong side of four black 2" squares. Place a marked square on a corner of a white 9½" square, making sure the corners and sides of the white and black squares are aligned. Sew along the marked line and trim, leaving ¼" seam allowances. Repeat on the other three corners of the white square, making a Snowball block. Press the seam allowances toward the black triangles. Repeat to make a total of 12 Snowball blocks.

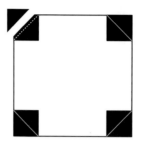 

Make 12.

2. Using your preferred appliqué method (I used the freezer-paper method described on page 25), prepare a large circle A from one of the black, yellow, or black-and-white prints. Center and appliqué the fabric circle on a Snowball block. I appliquéd my circles by machine with monofilament using a blind hem stitch. You can appliqué by hand or machine. Repeat to make a total of 12 large-circle appliqué blocks.

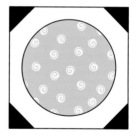

Make 12.

3. Repeat step 1 using four yellow-and-white 4¼" squares on a white 9½" square. Press the seam allowances toward the yellow triangles. Make 20 blocks.

Make 20.

4. Using your preferred appliqué method, prepare a small circle B from one of the black, yellow, or black-and-white prints. Center and appliqué the fabric circle on a block from step 3. Repeat to make a total of 20 small-circle appliqué blocks.

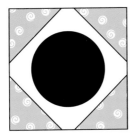

Make 20.

Freezer-Paper Appliqué

I use freezer paper when preparing my appliqué shapes.

1. Trace the pattern onto the dull side of the freezer paper and cut it out along the line.
2. Using a bit of glue stick, adhere the paper shape to the wrong side of the appliqué fabric, shiny side facing up.
3. Cut out, leaving about ¼" seam allowance beyond the edge of the paper circle, and press the seam allowances to the shiny side of the paper.
4. Position the piece on your background and stitch by hand or machine.
5. After stitching, carefully cut away the background fabric and remove the freezer paper.

ASSEMBLING THE QUILT TOP

1. Lay out the blocks in nine rows of seven blocks each, as shown in the quilt assembly diagram on page 26. Note the placement of appliquéd blocks and the orientation of the pieced blocks. Odd rows contain the small-circle appliqué blocks alternated with the pieced blocks oriented so that the white strip is horizontal. Even rows contain the large-circle appliqué blocks alternated with the pieced blocks oriented so that the white strip is vertical.

2. Sew the blocks together into rows. Press the seam allowances toward the pieced blocks to make it easier to match seams between rows.

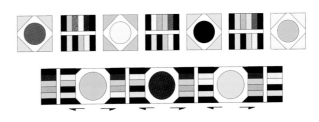

Pin for Precision

Pin where the white strip of the pieced blocks matches the white background of the small-circle appliqué blocks. The width of the white strip should equal the width of the white background at the seam lines.

3. Sew the rows together, pinning at key intersections. Press the seam allowances open. The quilt center should measure 63½" x 81½".

ADDING BORDERS AND FINISHING THE QUILT

Measure your quilt before trimming border strips to the specified length. Refer to the quilt assembly diagram as you add the borders. If you need more information on adding borders or finishing, visit ShopMartingale.com/HowtoQuilt.

1. To make the pieced border, draw a diagonal line from corner to corner on the wrong side of two black 2" squares. Place a marked square at one end of a white 2" x 9½" rectangle. Sew along the marked line and trim, leaving ¼" seam allowance. Press the seam allowances toward the black triangle. Repeat on the other end of the white rectangle to make unit A. Make a total of 14 units.

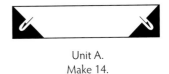

Unit A.
Make 14.

2. Draw a diagonal line from corner to corner on the wrong side of each white 2" square. Place a marked square at the left end of a black 2" x 11" rectangle. Sew along the marked line and trim, leaving ¼" seam allowances to make unit B. Press the seam allowances toward the black strip. Make two units.

Unit B.
Make 2.

3. Place a marked square at the right end of a black 2" x 11" rectangle. Sew along the marked line and trim, leaving ¼" seam allowances to make unit C. Press the seam allowances toward the black rectangle. Make two units.

Unit C.
Make 2.

4. For the left and right borders, lay out five black 2" x 9½" rectangles and four of unit A as shown. Sew the pieces together end to end and press the seam allowances toward the black rectangles. Make two and sew the pieced border strips to the left and right sides of the quilt center. *Note:* Line up the black triangles with the black strips of the pieced blocks; pin so they don't shift when sewing. Press the seam allowances toward the pieced border.

Make 2.

5. For the top and bottom borders, lay out one unit B, three of unit A, two black 2" x 9½" rectangles, and one unit C as shown. Sew the pieces together end to end and press the seam allowances toward the black rectangles. Make two. Join the pieced border strips to the top and bottom of the quilt center. Line up the black triangles with the black strips of the pieced blocks and pin as before. Press the seam allowances toward the pieced borders. The quilt should now measure 66½" x 84½".

Make 2.

6. Sew eight white 2" x 42" strips together end to end; press the seam allowances open. Cut two strips 66½" long. Sew the strips to the top and bottom of the quilt; press the seam allowances toward the white borders. From the remaining strip, cut two strips 87½" long. Sew the strips to the left and right sides of the quilt. Press the seam allowances toward the white borders.

7. Sew four black 2½" x 42" strips together end to end; press the seam allowances open. Cut two strips 69½" long. Sew the strips to the top and bottom of the quilt; press the seam allowances toward the black borders.

8. Sew five black 2½" x 42" strips together end to end; press the seam allowances open. Cut two strips 91½" long. Sew the strips to the left and right sides of the quilt. Press the seam allowances toward the black borders. The quilt top should now measure 73½" x 91½".

Quilt assembly

9. Piece the quilt backing and prepare the binding. Layer and baste the backing, batting, and quilt top. Quilt as desired and bind your quilt.

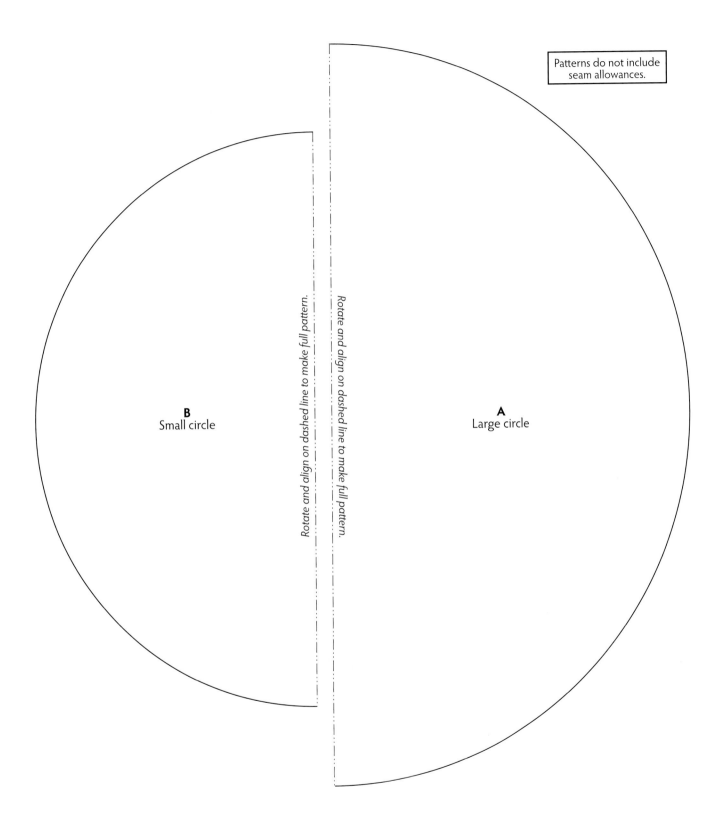

B
Small circle

A
Large circle

Rotate and align on dashed line to make full pattern.

Rotate and align on dashed line to make full pattern.

Patterns do not include seam allowances.

After making the planned version in black, white, and yellow, I knew immediately that I wanted to make the quilt again. I had a Jelly Roll plus some yardage from Minick and Simpson's Wiscasset fabric line for Moda. I realized that I could use the Jelly Roll strips to make the pieced alternate blocks; this resulted in larger but fewer blocks and a larger quilt. With several nieces and nephews yet to get married, this queen-size quilt just might be the perfect wedding gift for one of them.

Since the blocks were now 12" instead of 9", I decided to cut the circles from pieced four-patch units to add a bit more fabric variety. Plus the "cheater cloth" I used for the smaller appliquéd circles fools the eye into thinking the teardrops are appliquéd as well. I also wanted a different border from the planned version. Most fabric lines have a few fabrics that include all of the colors in a larger print, making them a perfect choice for a final outer border.

Pieced by Nancy Allen; machine quilted by Sue Baddley with a digitized design
Finished quilt: 84½" x 108½" • **Finished block:** 12" x 12"

This make-do version is a wall quilt with 6" blocks. The pieced blocks are made from 1½"-wide strips. Although the quilt uses a wide variety of fabrics, I tried to keep the color tones and values consistent. For example, with very few exceptions, the light background fabrics are all beiges—no whites. The colored prints are primarily medium values, so the beige backgrounds and the black strips stand out to create the secondary pattern in the quilt.

Since the strips and blocks are smaller than in the planned and coordinated versions, I chose fabrics with small prints to match the scale of the quilt. My goal was to make this quilt completely from my scrap bag and not purchase any new fabric for the quilt top. I was able to do this by making a scrappy piano-key border rather than using a single fabric. Note that even the light and dark inner borders are made of scraps.

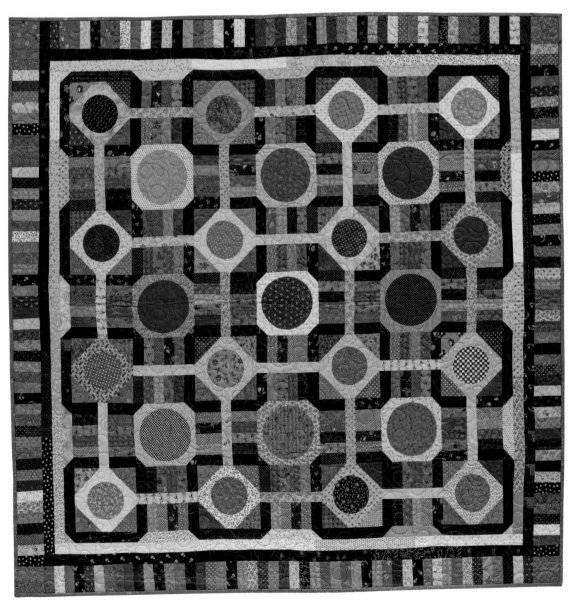

Pieced by Nancy Allen; machine quilted by Sue Baddley with a meandering design
Finished quilt: 54½" x 54½" • Finished block: 6" x 6"

Plaza Mayor

Pieced by Nancy Allen; machine quilted by Catherine Timmons with a meandering design
Finished quilt: 62" x 75½" • Finished block: 12" x 12"

I lived in Madrid, Spain, as a college student and later as a graduate teaching assistant, and I've returned to visit Spain many times since. My favorite location in Madrid is the Plaza Mayor—and of course the famed Sobrino de Botín and Casa Paco restaurants and the many tapas cuevas *(caves) that surround the plaza. Although this design wasn't originally inspired by the Plaza Mayor, the completed quilt reminded me of the concrete and stone design on the ground of the popular plaza, and the name seemed perfect. This is a great beginner quilt because of the simple piecing.*

The Make-Do Quilt

This make-do version, unlike the planned and coordinated versions, uses many fabrics in each block. Each of the nine large squares in each block is a different fabric. The more, the merrier, I say. However, I used the same fabric for the four small squares and the light vertical and horizontal pieces in each block. You could certainly scrap up the lights, and the result would be fabulous.

No fat quarters were harmed to make this project! I was very random as I selected fabrics for the blocks. I started by going through my scraps and selecting every piece from which I could cut a 3½" square. Next I went through previously cut fat quarters to get additional 3½" squares. Then I went through my miscellaneous 2"-wide strips to cut the four matching small squares in each block.

This version also uses a single fabric for the sashing, rather than pieced sashing as in the other variations. With the exception of the border, this quilt came entirely from my stash and scrap bag. Since my scraps are mostly medium and dark fabrics, I used black to frame the blocks.

MATERIALS

Yardage is based on 42"-wide fabric unless otherwise noted.

2⅛ yards *total* of medium and dark prints for blocks
2 yards of black floral for outer border*
1⅜ yards *total* of light prints for blocks
1⅛ yards of small-scale black print for sashing and inner border
⅔ yard of fabric for binding
4⅔ yards of fabric for backing
70" x 84" piece of batting

*This yardage allows for borders to be cut from the lengthwise grain. If you prefer to cut crosswise and piece the outer border, 1 yard of fabric is enough.

CUTTING

From the medium and dark prints, cut:
180 squares, 3½" x 3½"
20 sets of 4 matching squares, 2" x 2" (80 total)

From the light prints, cut:
20 sets of 12 matching rectangles, 2" x 3½" (240 total)

From the small-scale black print, cut:
18 strips, 2" x 42"; crosscut *5 of the strips* into
    15 rectangles, 2" x 12½"

From the black floral, cut *lengthwise*:
4 strips, 3½" x 72"

From the binding fabric, cut:
8 strips, 2¼" x 42"

MAKING THE BLOCKS

1. Select nine 3½" squares from assorted fabrics, one set of 12 matching light 2" x 3½" rectangles, and one set of four matching medium or dark 2" squares. Lay out the block as shown.

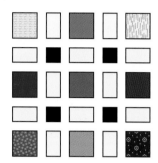

2. I suggest that you chain piece this block together. It makes the sewing go quickly. Join the first two pieces in the first row. Then, without snipping the threads, sew the first two pieces in the second row. Continue for all five rows of the block. Remove the five units from the machine, but do not snip the threads between the rows. Add the next piece in each row and continue in this manner until each row is stitched together and each of the rows is held together by threads at each seam. Press seam allowances in opposite directions from row to row. You can press after sewing pieces together, or wait until all the rows are sewn.

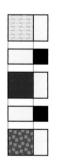 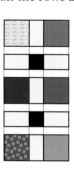 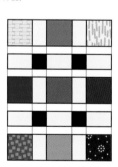

Sew first 2 pieces in each row.   Add the next piece.   Complete the rows.

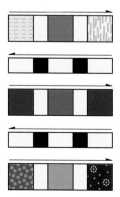

3. Sew the rows together, pinning at each of the seams to ensure they remain aligned. Press the seam allowances in one direction. The block will measure 12½" square.

4. Repeat steps 1–3 to make a total of 20 blocks.

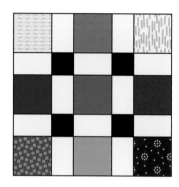

Make 20.

ASSEMBLING THE QUILT TOP

1. Lay out the blocks in five rows of four blocks each. Add a black-print 2" x 12½" sashing rectangle between the blocks in each row. When you're happy with the arrangement, sew the blocks and sashing rectangles together in rows.

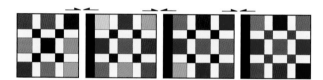

Make 5 rows.

2. Sew six black-print 2" x 42" strips together end to end. Press the seam allowances open and cross-cut into four strips 53" long. *Note:* Measure your rows first; if they do not measure 53", take an average of the five rows and cut the sashing strips to that length. Sew the rows and sashing strips together and press the seam allowances toward the sashing. The quilt center should now measure 53" x 66½".

ADDING BORDERS AND FINISHING THE QUILT

Measure your quilt through the center before trimming border strips to the specified lengths. If you need more information on adding borders or finishing your quilt, visit ShopMartingale.com/HowtoQuilt.

1. Sew seven black-print 2" x 42" strips together end to end for the inner border. Press the seam allowances open and crosscut into two strips 66½" long and two strips 56" long. Refer to the quilt assembly diagram below as you add the borders.

2. Sew the longer strips to the sides of the quilt and the shorter strips to the top and bottom. Press the seam allowances toward the inner border.

3. Trim two black-floral 3½" x 72" strips to 69½" long for the side borders and two to 62" long for the top and bottom borders.

4. Sew the side borders to the quilt, and then add the top and bottom borders. Press the seam allowances toward the outer border. The quilt should now measure 62" x 75½".

5. Piece the quilt backing and prepare the binding. Layer and baste the backing, batting, and quilt top. Quilt as desired and bind your quilt.

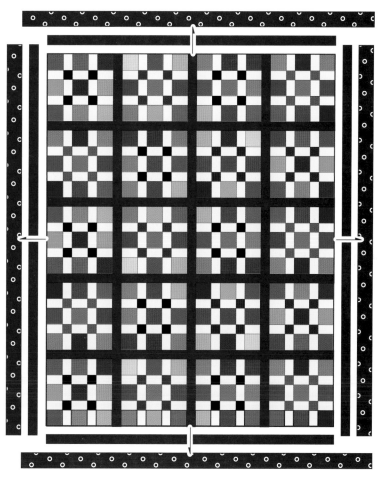

Quilt assembly

I love the comfy, cozy appeal of quilts using home-spun plaids. I wanted this quilt to have an old-fashioned, utilitarian feel, so I even included my test blocks that used slightly different-sized pieces. This would be a great picnic quilt, especially since I backed it with a thick flannel fabric. It would also be a perfect candidate for hand quilting using a folk-arty big stitch.

Don't get hung up on cutting the plaids perfectly. If the plaids are cut just a little off-kilter it only adds to the primitive charm. Homespuns don't have a right or wrong side. However, some might be brushed on one side and have a flannel-like feel. I don't worry about whether the brushed or nonbrushed side is on top; the slight texture variation will provide added interest to this old-fashioned quilt.

You can certainly mix the homespun plaids with other fabrics as I did for the sashing. I felt that using the more tightly woven fabrics in the sashing would add stability to the homespun fabrics, which are often more loosely woven.

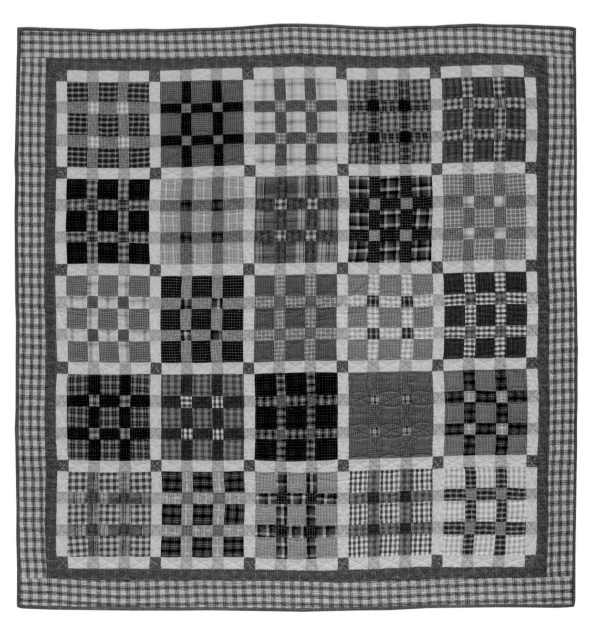

Pieced by Nancy Allen; custom machine quilted by Catherine Timmons
Finished quilt: 64½" x 64½" • Finished block: 9½" x 9½"

When I fall in love with an entire line of fabrics, I splurge on a complete fat-quarter pack—rather than just precut squares and strips. That was the case with this French General fabric called Maison de Garance. I especially love the rhythm created by the striped fabric used in the pieced sashing.

For this quilt, I used a layered cutting method. I started with 16" squares cut from 20 of my favorite fat quarters. (I'll merge the remaining fat quarters into my stash, and they'll show up in future quilts—nothing goes to waste.) Four quilt blocks can be cut quickly by layering four fabric squares and making the cuts through all of the layers at once. The result is four ready-to-sew blocks. (For a make-do version, you can mix and match the squares to make scrappy blocks.)

Pieced by Nancy Allen; machine quilted by Sue Baddley with a digitized design
Finished quilt: 72½" x 87½" • Finished block: 13½" x 13½"

Best Friends Forever

Pieced by Nancy Allen; quilted by Sue Baddley with a digitized design
Finished quilt: 64½" x 64½" • **Finished block:** 9" x 9"

This quilt uses a variation of an Ohio Star block, changing the color and value so a friendship star appears in the foreground (hence the name of the quilt) and an octagon frames the star. Although this is a traditional block, it lends itself to all styles of fabrics. For each of my three variations, I selected fabrics with enough contrast that the star points show up clearly. If I'm going to the trouble of matching points, I want all of that precision piecing work to be obvious!

The Make-Do Quilt

It's easy to get into a color and fabric rut, even if you make scrappy quilts. To try something different, select a unique background fabric—something in an unexpected color (such as olive green, which will read as a neutral in the quilt) or an interesting print with a neutral background to provide added visual interest. You can also make this quilt even scrappier by using a variety of background fabrics.

MATERIALS

Yardage is based on 42"-wide fabric unless otherwise noted.

3 yards *total* of at least 25 assorted light, medium, and dark prints for blocks and pieced border

1⅜ yards of background fabric for blocks and pieced border

1¼ yards of dark-blue fabric for second and fourth borders

⅜ yard of red print for first border

⅝ yard of fabric for binding

4⅛ yards of fabric for backing

73" x 73" piece of batting

CUTTING

For each block, you'll need three different prints in addition to the background fabric: fabric A for the "octagon" background, fabric B for the star-points background, and fabric C for the foreground star.

From the background fabric, cut:
5 strips, 3⅞" x 42"; crosscut into 50 squares, 3⅞" x 3⅞"*
4 strips, 5" x 42"; crosscut into 30 squares, 5" x 5"*
4 squares, 4" x 4"

From *each of 25* assorted prints (fabric A), cut:
2 squares, 3⅞" x 3⅞"
1 square, 4¼" x 4¼"; cut into quarters diagonally to yield 4 quarter-square triangles

From *each of 25* assorted prints (fabric B), cut:
1 square, 4¼" x 4¼"; cut into quarters diagonally to yield 4 quarter-square triangles

From *each of 25* assorted prints (fabric C), cut:
1 square, 3½" x 3½"
2 squares, 3⅞" x 3⅞"; cut squares in half diagonally to yield 4 half-square triangles

From the assorted prints, cut:
30 squares, 5" x 5"*

From the red print, cut:
5 strips, 2" x 42"; cut *1* strip into 4 equal rectangles, 2" x approximately 10½"

From the dark-blue fabric, cut:
12 strips, 2¾" x 42"

From the binding fabric, cut:
7 strips, 2¼" x 42"

Allows for squaring up hourglass units.

MAKING THE BLOCKS

The instructions are written for making one block at a time.

1. Select two fabric A 3⅞" squares and two background-fabric 3⅞" squares. Refer to "Starting with Squares" on page 16. Make four

half-square-triangle units. Press the seam allowances toward the background triangles.

Make 4.

2. Select a fabric A quarter-square triangle that matches the fabric from step 1 and sew it to a fabric B quarter-square triangle as shown. Press the seam allowances toward the fabric B triangle. Note that you are aligning the two corners with the 90° angles. Make four.

Make 4.

3. Sew a fabric C half-square triangle to each of the units from step 2. Press the seam allowances toward the C triangle. Make four.

Make 4.

4. Lay out the units from steps 1 and 3 and the matching fabric C 3½" square to make the block as shown. Sew the units into rows. Press the center-row seam allowances toward the center square and press the seam allowances in the top and bottom rows open. Sew the rows together, pinning where seams intersect. Press the seam allowances open.

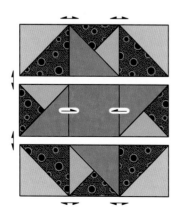

5. Follow steps 1–4 to make a total of 25 blocks. Blocks should measure 9½" square.

ASSEMBLING THE QUILT TOP

1. Lay out the blocks in five rows of five blocks each. When you're happy with the arrangement, sew the blocks in each row together, carefully matching and pinning the star points between blocks before sewing. Press the seam allowances open.
2. Sew the rows together, carefully matching and pinning the star points and seams between rows. Press the seam allowances open. The quilt center should now measure 45½" x 45½".

ADDING BORDERS AND FINISHING THE QUILT

Refer to the quilt assembly diagram on page 39 as you add the borders. If you need more information on adding borders or finishing your quilt, visit ShopMartingale.com/HowtoQuilt.

1. Sew a red-print 2" x 42" strip to a red-print 2" x 10½" rectangle end to end. Press the seam allowances open. Make four border strips. Trim the two side border strips to 45½" long. Trim the two top and bottom border strips to 48½" long.
2. Sew the side borders to the left and right sides of the quilt center, and then add the top and bottom borders. Press all seam allowances toward the red borders. The quilt should now measure 48½" x 48½".
3. Sew five dark-blue 2¾" x 42" strips together end to end. Press the seam allowances open. Cut two border strips 48½" long and two border strips 53" long.
4. Sew the shorter strips to opposite sides of the quilt; press the seam allowances toward the dark-blue borders. Sew the longer border strips to the top and bottom of the quilt. Press the seam allowances toward the dark-blue borders. The quilt should now measure 53" x 53".

5. To make the pieced border, select one background 5" square and one print 5" square. Refer to "Making Hourglass Units" on page 19 to make an hourglass unit. Press the seam allowances in one direction. Repeat to make a total of 60 hourglass units. Square each unit to 4" x 4".

Make 60.

6. Sew 15 hourglass units together to make a border strip, rotating every other hourglass unit. Press the seam allowances open. Make four border strips. Sew borders to the left and right sides of the quilt center; press the seam allowances toward the dark-blue border.

Make 4.

7. Sew a background 4" square to each end of the two remaining hourglass border units. Press the seam allowances toward the corner squares. Sew the border units to the top and bottom of the quilt center. Press the seam allowances toward the dark-blue border. The quilt should now measure 60" x 60".

Make 2.

8. Join seven dark-blue 2¾" x 42" strips end to end. Press the seam allowances open. Cut two border strips 60" long for the side borders and two border strips 64½" long for the top and bottom borders.

9. Sew the side borders to the quilt and press the seam allowances toward the dark-blue borders. Sew the remaining borders to the top and bottom of the quilt and press. The quilt should now measure 64½" x 64½".

10. Piece the quilt backing and prepare the binding. Layer and baste the backing, batting, and quilt top. Quilt as desired and bind your quilt.

Quilt assembly

For a long time I wanted to make an Amish-style quilt, that is, a quilt with a black background and vivid solid colors. If you need to make a quilt on a budget, choosing solid fabrics is a great option, because they're usually about half the price of prints. I decided to keep the border very simple in keeping with this "plain and fancy" quilt. I wanted aqua to be the predominant color, in addition to the black background, so I repeated it in the borders. My quilt has two blocks each in burgundy, yellow, tan, orange, aqua, red, and purple, plus three blocks each of blue and green.

This is the only version of "Best Friends Forever" that has sashing. I like the design formed by the black sashing and black in the blocks. Also, by adding sashing, you don't need to match star points between blocks, which makes sewing the rows together much easier. My quilter used a variegated thread that worked beautifully against the variety of solid fabrics.

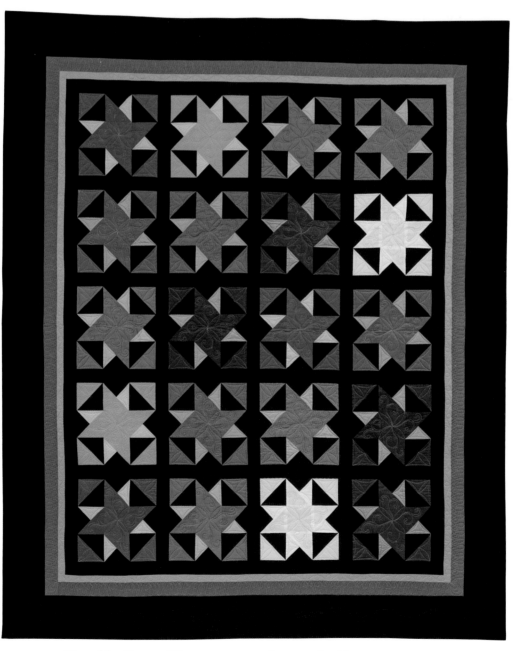

Pieced by Nancy Allen; custom machine quilted by Jen Alexander
Finished quilt: 76½" x 90½" • Finished block: 12" x 12"

The Best Friends Forever design works equally well with the classic French country–style Breath of Avignon fabrics by American Jane for Moda. It started with one Layer Cake (10" squares) and two charm packs (5" squares). The quilt also includes three background fabrics from the fabric line, the cream-and-red light print for the blocks and borders, as well as a medium-green and a medium-blue fabric to create the octagon shapes framing the stars.

Simply select 36 Layer Cake squares and group them into 18 pairs. Each pair of fabrics will be used in two blocks, with one fabric as the foreground star and the other fabric as the background star points in one block, and then vice versa for a companion block. The block size for this coordinated version is the same as the make-do version. You'll end up with one extra block, which gives you some flexibility when you lay out the blocks. Combine half of the pairs with the green coordinated quarter-square triangles (for the octagon background) and the remaining pairs with the blue coordinated fabric. Then use the charm packs and scraps to make the piano-key border. The inner and outer borders each finish 3" wide and the piano-key border finishes 4½" wide.

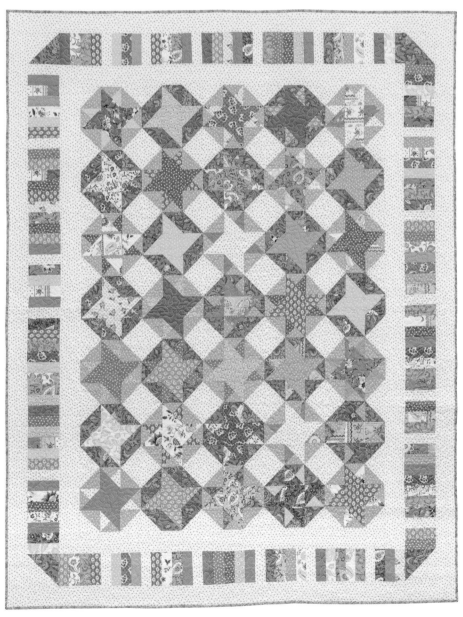

Pieced by Nancy Allen; quilted by Catherine Timmons with a meandering design
Finished quilt: 66½" x 84½" • Finished block: 9" x 9"

Bricks and Cobblestones

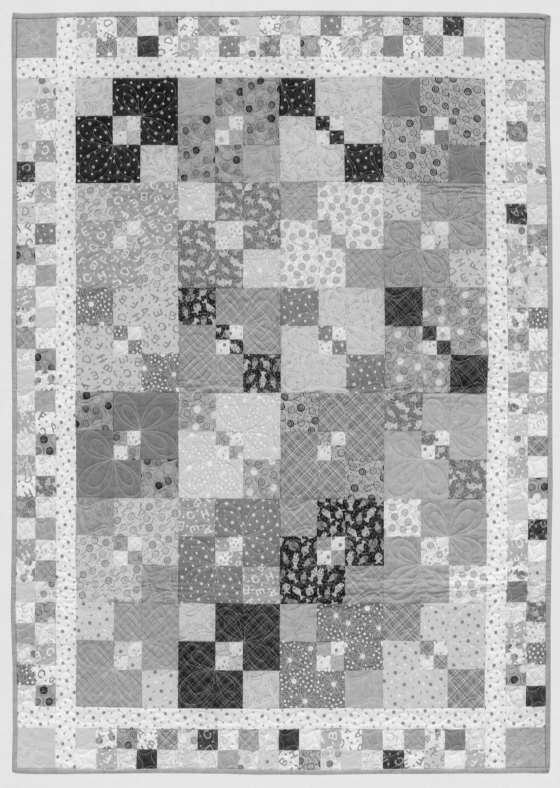

Pieced by Nancy Allen; custom machine quilted by Jen Alexander

Finished quilt: 39½" x 54½" • **Finished block:** 7½" x 7½"

The Bricks and Cobblestones pattern is the perfect example of how different the same quilt block can look when you vary the fabric and value placement. It's almost hard to tell that the three quilt variations are all from the same simple block.

The Coordinated Quilt

This is a great option for a crib quilt—and all you'll need is one pack of precut 10" squares, one charm pack, and a little yardage for the inner border . . . and, of course, backing and binding. Mix and match 24 of the 10" squares into pairs, which will be subcut and used for two companion blocks. You can certainly mix it up for more variety. The rest of the 10" squares will be combined with charm-pack squares for the checkerboard border.

MATERIALS

Yardage is based on 42"-wide fabric unless otherwise noted.

1 precut pack of 40 squares, 10" x 10", for blocks and checkerboard border
1 charm pack (40 squares, 5" x 5") for checkerboard border and border corner squares
½ yard of light print for inner border
½ yard of fabric for binding
3 yards of fabric for backing
48" x 62" piece of batting

CUTTING

Select 24 of the 10" squares for blocks and three light 10" squares for the four-patch units in the center of the blocks. Choose seven of the 10" squares, in combination with charm squares, for the checkerboard border.

From *each of 24* medium to dark 10" squares, cut:*
2 strips, 3¼" x 10"; crosscut *each* strip into:
    1 square, 3¼" x 3¼" (2 total)
    1 rectangle, 3¼" x 5¼" (2 total)
    1 rectangle, 1½" x 3¼" (2 total; 1 is extra)
1 strip, 2½" x 10"; crosscut into 2 rectangles, 2½" x 3¼"

From *3 light* 10" squares, cut *a total of:*
8 strips, 1½" x 10"; crosscut into 24 rectangles, 1½" x 3¼"

From *each of 7* of the 10" squares, cut:
2 strips, 2" x 10"; crosscut *each* strip into 2 rectangles, 2" x 5" (28 total)

From *each of 4* charm squares, cut:
1 square, 3½" x 3½" (4 total)

From *each of 36* charm squares, cut:
2 rectangles, 2" x 5" (72 total)

From the light print, cut:
3 strips, 2" x 42"
2 strips, 2" x 42"; crosscut *each* strip into:
    1 strip, 2" x 30½"
    2 rectangles, 2" x 3½"

From the binding fabric, cut:
5 strips, 2¼" x 42"

*Refer to the cutting guide below when cutting these pieces.

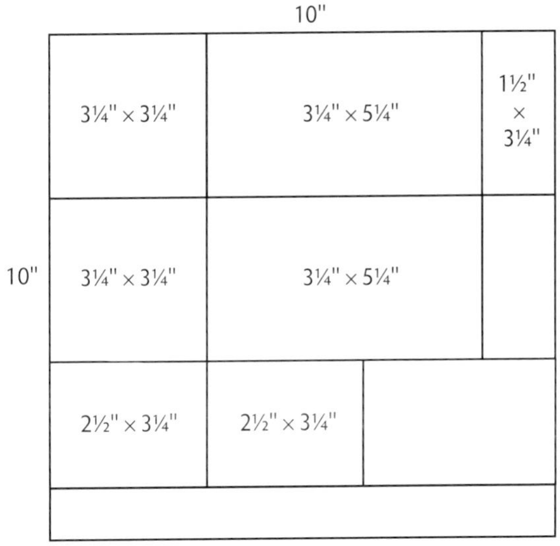

10"		
3¼" × 3¼"	3¼" × 5¼"	1½" × 3¼"
3¼" × 3¼"	3¼" × 5¼"	
2½" × 3¼"	2½" × 3¼"	

Cutting guide

MAKING THE BLOCKS

1. Pair a medium or dark 1½" x 3¼" rectangle with a light 1½" x 3¼" rectangle and sew them together along the 3¼" sides. Press the seam allowances toward the medium/dark fabric. Cut the strip into two segments, 1½" wide. Sew the two segments into a four-patch unit. Press the seam allowances to one side, or spin the seam allowances as shown on page 16.

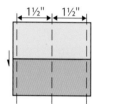

2. Using the unit from step 1, two 3¼" squares that match the unit from step 1, and a matching set of two 2½" x 3¼" rectangles and two 3¼" x 5¼" rectangles, lay out the block as shown. Note the orientation of the center four-patch unit. Sew the pieces together in rows; press the seam allowances toward the rectangles. Match the seams and sew the rows together.

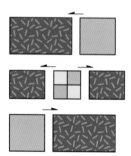 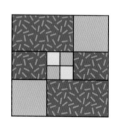

Press Later

Wait to press the horizontal seams of the block until you've laid out the blocks and know which ones will be next to each other. Then press every other block toward the four-patch unit and the alternates away from the four-patch unit.

3. Repeat steps 1 and 2 to make a total of 24 blocks. Blocks should measure 8" square.

ASSEMBLING THE QUILT

1. Lay out the blocks in six rows of four blocks each. When you're happy with the arrangement, press the horizontal block seam allowances in opposite directions from block to block.

2. Join the blocks in each row together, pressing the seam allowances in opposite directions from row to row. Pin the rows together at the opposing seams and sew the rows together. Press the seam allowances in one direction. The quilt top should now measure 30½" x 45½".

ADDING BORDERS AND FINISHING THE QUILT

Refer to the quilt assembly diagram on page 45 as you add the borders. If you need more information on adding borders or finishing, visit ShopMartingale.com/HowtoQuilt.

1. Sew the light-print 2" x 30½" strips to the top and bottom of the quilt. Press the seam allowances toward the light-print border. Note that you will attach the horizontal checkerboard border before you attach the side inner borders.

2. Pair a light 2" x 5" rectangle with a darker 2" x 5" rectangle. Sew along the 5" sides to make a strip set. Press the seam allowances toward the darker fabric. Make 50 strip sets. Crosscut each strip set into two segments, 2" wide, to make 100 two-patch units.

Make 50 strip sets.
Cut 100 segments.

3. Arrange the two-patch units and sew into two border strips with 20 two-patch units each and two border strips with 30 two-patch units each. Sew shorter border strips to the top and bottom of the quilt. Press the seam allowances toward the light inner border.

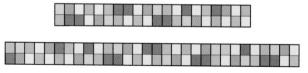

Make 2 of each.

4. Sew three light-print 2" x 42" strips together end to end and press the seam allowance open. Cut two strips 54½" long. Sew the border strips to the left and right sides of the quilt. Press the seam allowances toward the border.

5. Sew a light-print 2" x 3½" rectangle to each end of the remaining checkerboard borders from step 3. Press the seam allowances toward the light rectangles. Sew a medium or dark 3½" square to each end of the borders and press the seam allowances toward the corner squares.

6. Sew border units to the left and right sides of the quilt and press the seam allowances toward the light inner border. Stay stitch about ⅛" in from the edge around the quilt. The quilt should now measure 39½" x 54½".

7. Piece the quilt backing and prepare the binding. Layer and baste the backing, batting, and quilt top. Quilt as desired and bind your quilt.

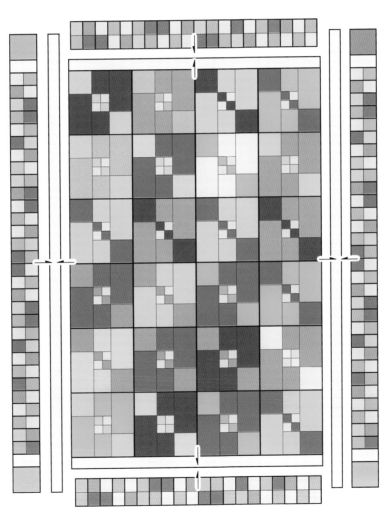

Quilt assembly

While this is a beginner-level quilt, you'll need to pay close attention to fabric placement, because adjoining blocks use matching fabrics to create this variation in the design. I found it easiest to first cut out all of the fabrics, and then work row by row. I sewed the four-patch units (the "cobblestones") that are the center section of each block and used them as my guide for which fabrics went into each block.

As you complete each block, lay it out on your design wall—or if you are like me, on your "design floor." The inner border finishes 2" wide, the checkerboard-border squares finish 2" x 2", and the outer-border squares finish 4" x 4". I used three light batiks throughout the quilt, but you could make it scrappier by using many different light batiks.

Pieced by Nancy Allen; quilted by Catherine Timmons with a meandering design
Finished quilt: 80½" x 100½" • Finished block: 10" x 10"

Although the make-do version of "Bricks and Cobblestones" uses a variety of fabrics pulled from my scraps, I used the same black and light fabrics in each of the center four-patch "cobblestone" units. This gives the blocks a common element, which both unifies the blocks and gives your eye a familiar place to settle as you look at the quilt. You could rotate every other block for a more random look, but I like the repetition of the horizontal rows when the blocks are all set the same direction. The inner rust-striped border finishes 2½" wide, the squares in the checker-board border finish 1½" x 1½", and the outer border finishes 5" wide. I used the same rust-striped fabric to bind the quilt.

Pieced by Nancy Allen; machine quilted by Sue Baddley with a digitized design

Finished quilt: 61½" x 61½" • **Finished block:** 10" x 10"

Days of '47

Pieced by Nancy Allen; custom machine quilted by Catherine Timmons

Finished quilt: 61½" x 61½" • **Finished block:** 10" x 10"

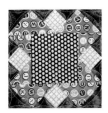

This quilt features the not-so-familiar Salt Lake City block. I've long wanted to make a quilt featuring this block to honor my Mormon pioneer ancestors, especially my great-great-grandfather, who entered the Salt Lake Valley in 1847, just two months after Brigham Young's original pioneer company arrived. They arrived to nothing but mountains and desert. Within a couple of years their hard work made the valley "blossom as a rose." I added sashing between the blocks in each version. It not only represents Salt Lake City's street grid system, but it also simplifies the quilt assembly, because you won't have to worry about matching points on all sides of the blocks. The large center square in the block is an opportunity to feature a favorite large-scale print.

The Coordinated Quilt

The coordinated "Days of '47" quilt uses Circa 1934 fabrics by Cosmo Cricket for Moda. I couldn't resist using a black print from the collection as the block background and in the border. The use of a dark background shows off the unique piecing in the block. Plus, a secondary shoofly design emerges at the block corners when the same dark fabric is used in the corners of all blocks and in the sashing cornerstones.

MATERIALS

Yardage is based on 42"-wide fabric unless otherwise noted.

2 yards *total* of at least 16 assorted prints for blocks*
2 yards of multicolored print for outer border**
1¾ yards of cream solid for sashing, inner border, and pieced border
1 yard of black tone-on-tone print for block background, sashing squares, and pieced border
⅝ yard of fabric for binding
4 yards of fabric for backing
70" x 70" piece of batting

A fat-eighth bundle of a complete fabric line will give you plenty of coordinated prints to mix and match. It will be more fabric than needed, but will offer flexibility when piecing your blocks.
**If you prefer to piece your border rather than use a lengthwise cut, you will need only 1 yard.*

CUTTING

From the assorted prints, cut *a total of*:
16 squares, 5½" x 5½"
16 sets of 4 matching squares, 2¼" x 2¼"

From *each of 16* of the assorted prints, cut:
1 square, 6¼" x 6¼"; cut into quarters diagonally to yield 4 quarter-square triangles
2 squares, 3⅜" x 3⅜"; cut in half diagonally to yield 4 half-square triangles

From the black tone-on-tone print, cut:
4 strips, 3¾" x 42"; crosscut into 32 squares, 3¾" x 3¾". Cut each square into quarters diagonally to yield 128 quarter-square triangles.
3 strips, 3⅜" x 42"; crosscut into 32 squares, 3⅜" x 3⅜". Cut each square in half diagonally to yield 64 half-square triangles.
3 strips, 2¼" x 42"; crosscut into 40 squares, 2¼" x 2¼"
1 strip, 2" x 42"; crosscut into 9 squares, 2" x 2"

From the cream solid, cut *lengthwise*:
4 strips, 3¼" x 54"; crosscut into:
    2 strips, 3¼" x 45"
    2 strips, 3¼" x 50½"

From the remaining cream solid, cut:
24 rectangles, 2" x 10½"
40 squares, 3⅜" x 3⅜"; cut in half diagonally to yield 80 half-square triangles
4 squares, 3" x 3"

From the multicolored print, cut *lengthwise*:
4 strips, 3½" x 72"; crosscut into:
    2 strips, 3½" x 55½"
    2 strips, 3½" x 61½"

Continued on page 50

From the remaining multicolored print, cut:

20 squares, 3¾" x 3¾"; cut into quarters diagonally to yield 80 quarter-square triangles

From the binding fabric, cut:

7 strips, 2¼" x 42"

MAKING THE BLOCKS

1. Sew two black tone-on-tone quarter-square triangles to an assorted-print 2¼" square. Make four. Press the seam allowances toward the triangles.

Make 4.

Handy Gadget

Use a corner trimmer ruler and rotary cutter to trim the points off the triangles. This allows you to easily line up triangles with the corners of the square.

2. Sew two matching assorted half-square triangles to a pieced unit from step 1 as shown. Press the seam allowances toward the triangles just added. Make two. If necessary, trim this unit to 3" x 5½", making sure to leave ¼" seam allowance above and below the square.

Make 2.

3. Sew two matching assorted quarter-square triangles to a pieced triangle from step 1 as shown. Press seam allowances toward the triangles just added. Make two.

Make 2.

4. Sew the pieced rectangles from step 2 to opposite sides of a 5½" square. Press the seam allowances toward the square.

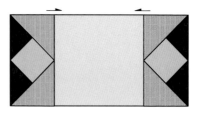

5. Sew the units from step 3 to the remaining sides; press the seam allowances open.

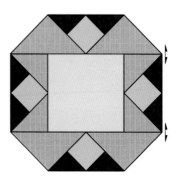

6. Sew a black tone-on-tone half-square triangle to each of the four corners. Press the seam allowances toward the corners. The block should measure 10½" square.

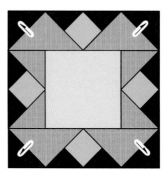

7. Repeat steps 1–6 to make a total of 16 blocks.

ASSEMBLING THE QUILT TOP

1. Lay out the blocks in four rows of four blocks each. Sew a cream 2" x 10½" sashing strip between the blocks in each row. Press the seam allowances toward the sashing.

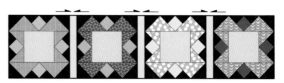

Make 4 rows.

2. Make a horizontal sashing row by joining four cream 2" x 10½" sashing strips and three black tone-on-tone 2" squares. Press the seam allowances toward the cream sashing strips. Make three rows.

Make 3.

3. Join the block rows and sashing rows as shown in the quilt assembly diagram below right. Press the seam allowances toward the sashing rows. The quilt center should now measure 45" x 45".

ADDING BORDERS AND FINISHING THE QUILT

1. Sew cream 3¼" x 45" border strips to the left and right sides of the quilt; press the seam allowances toward the borders. Sew cream 3¼" x 50½" border strips to the top and bottom of the quilt; press the seam allowances toward the borders. The quilt should now measure 50½" x 50½" square.

2. To make the pieced border, sew two multicolored-print quarter-square triangles to a black tone-on-tone 2¼" square. Press the seam allowances toward the triangles. Sew cream half-square triangles to the left and right sides of the pieced triangle. Press the seam allowances in opposite directions as shown. By pressing the seam allowances in this manner, you'll be able to "nest" the seams when you sew the units together in the next step. Make 40. If necessary, trim these units to 3" x 5½", making sure to leave ¼" seam allowances above and below the square.

Make 40.

3. Sew 10 pieced units together end to end. Press the seam allowances open. Make four pieced border strips. Sew cream 3" squares to both ends of two of the border strips. Press the seam allowances toward the corner squares.

Make 2.

Make 2.

4. Join border strips without corner squares to the left and right sides of the quilt center. Press the seam allowances toward the cream border. Join border strips with corner squares to the top and bottom of the quilt center and press toward the cream border. The quilt should now measure 55½" x 55½".

5. Sew multicolored 3½" x 55½" border strips to the left and right sides of the quilt and 3½" x 61½" border strips to the top and bottom of the quilt; press all seam allowances toward the outer borders. The quilt should now measure 61½" x 61½".

6. Piece the quilt backing and prepare the binding. Layer and baste the backing, batting, and quilt top. Quilt as desired and bind your quilt. If you need more information on finishing your quilt, visit ShopMartingale.com/HowtoQuilt.

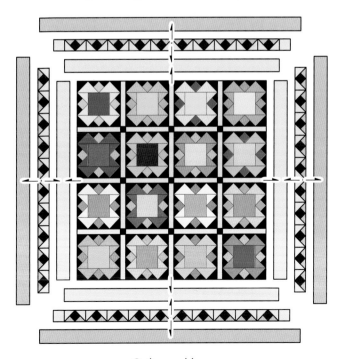

Quilt assembly

Who knew that red and aqua would look so great together? Until recently it wasn't a color scheme I'd seen, but with all of the fabulous red and aqua fabrics on the market, I knew I had to make a red-and-aqua quilt. While each block is a different mix of red and aqua prints, the quilt is unified by the large polka-dot block centers. The striped fabric and red corner squares create a nine-patch alternate pattern when the quilt is assembled with aqua sashing and red sashing squares. The striped fabric, the sashing, and the narrow borders all finish at 1¾" wide (cut 2¼" strips and squares). The outer border finishes at 5¼" wide.

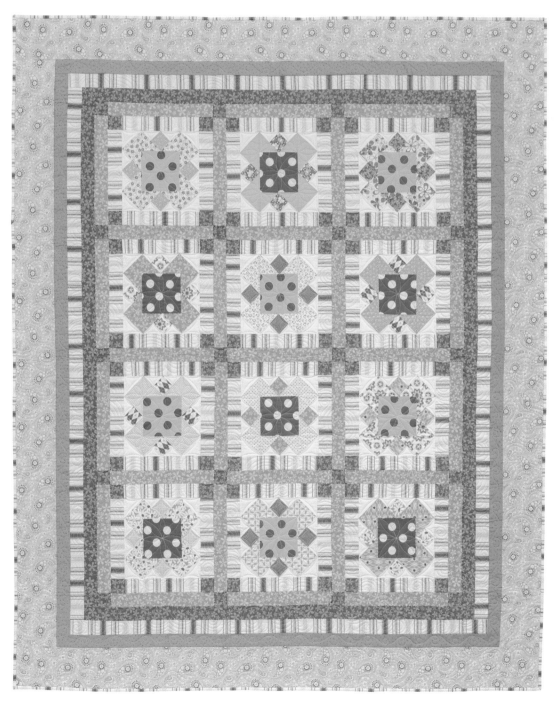

Pieced by Nancy Allen; custom machine quilted by Jen Alexander
Finished quilt: 68½" x 83¾" • **Finished block:** 10" x 10"

The **make-do version** of "Days of '47" is the perfect representation of my scrappy, make-do philosophy. I didn't fret about making all of the blocks match each other. In fact, there are fabrics in some blocks that actually clash with fabrics in other blocks. But the fabrics within each block work well with each other. I used sashing and border fabrics to unify the quilt. Although I used the same fabric for the sashing (which finishes 1¾" wide), I scrapped up the corner-stones, which helps your eyes move around the quilt.

My favorite part of this quilt is the addition of multiple narrow borders. The black-and-cream striped border finishes 1¾" wide, the narrower red-and-cream checked border finishes 1¼" wide, and the even narrower green border (using the same fabric as the sashing) finishes ¾" wide. The outer border is also a great example of my make-do philosophy. That fabric was leftover backing from a quilt I made a few years ago. With scrappy quilts, nothing goes to waste.

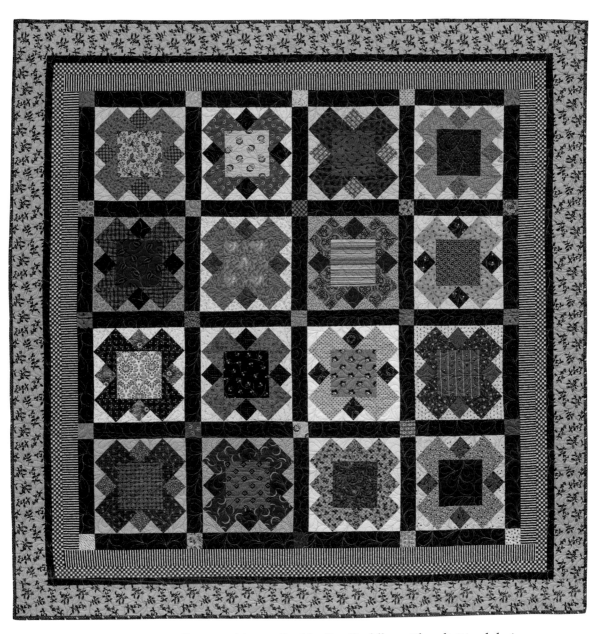

Pieced by Nancy Allen; machine quilted by Sue Baddley with a digitized design
Finished quilt: 63½" x 63¾" • Finished block: 10" x 10"

A Star Is Born

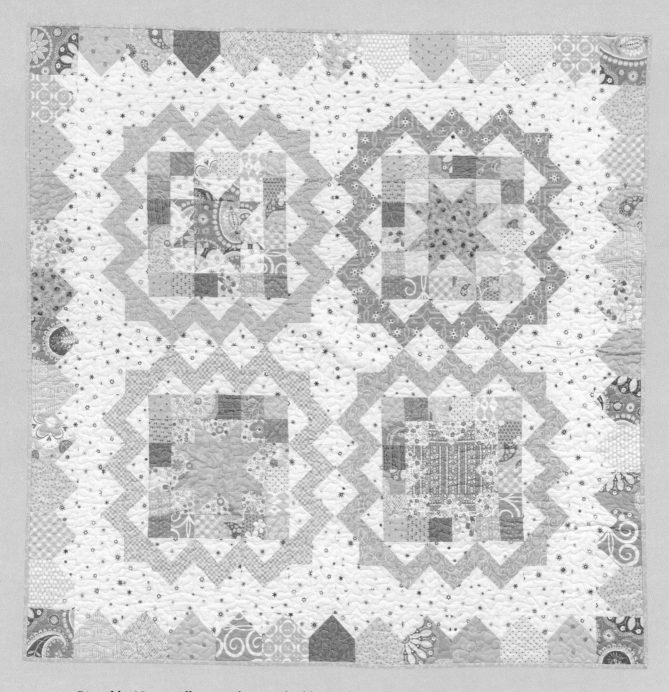

Pieced by Nancy Allen; machine quilted by Catherine Timmons with a meandering design
Finished quilt: 52½" x 52½" • Finished block: 20" x 20"

My favorite traditional quilt block to sew is the variable, eight-pointed star. I'm always trying to figure out new ways to incorporate that block into quilts. This year chevron designs have been popular in decorating and fashion, so I decided to incorporate the chevron design to highlight the Star block. And to have an excuse to use an even bigger variety of fabrics, I first framed the Star block with a patchwork border of squares.

The Planned Quilt

This quilt's planned pink, white, and lime-green color scheme began with the background fabric found on sale at clearance prices. (I bought all that the fabric store had.) Then I kept finding great pink, white, and lime-green prints until I had quite the collection. This planned quilt is my third quilt using this color scheme, and I'm not tired of it yet!

MATERIALS

Yardage is based on 42"-wide fabric unless otherwise noted.

2⅞ yards *total* of assorted pink and lime-green fabrics for blocks and outer border

2 yards of light print for blocks and borders

½ yard of fabric for binding

3½ yards of fabric for backing

61" x 61" piece of batting

CUTTING

From the pink and lime-green fabrics, cut *4 sets of*:

4 matching rectangles, 2½" x 4½", and 4 matching squares, 2½" x 2½" (for star background)

1 square, 4½" x 4½", and 8 matching squares, 2½" x 2½" (for star)

12 matching rectangles, 2½" x 4½", and 28 matching squares, 2½" x 2½" (for chevron ring)

From the remaining pink and lime-green fabrics, cut:

80 squares, 2½" x 2½"

48 squares, 4½" x 4½"

From the light print, cut:

26 strips, 2½" x 42"; crosscut *21* of the strips into:

64 rectangles, 2½" x 4¼"

200 squares, 2½" x 2½"

From the binding fabric, cut:

6 strips, 2¼" x 42"

MAKING THE BLOCKS

Select one set each of three different assorted pink and lime-green fabrics for each block—one set for the star, one for the star background, and one for the chevron ring.

1. Make four flying-geese units using the four matching 2½" x 4½" rectangles for the star background and the eight matching 2½" squares for the star. Refer to "Method 1: Squares and Rectangles" on page 18.

Make 4.

2. Sew a 2½" square for the star background to each end of two flying-geese units. Sew the remaining flying-geese units to opposite sides of the matching 4½" square. Press all seam allowances toward the squares. Sew the rows together and press the seam allowances open. The Star block should measure 8½" square.

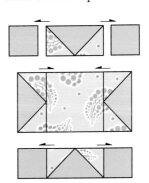 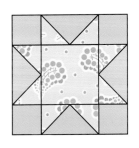

3. Sew four assorted 2½" squares together end to end; press the seam allowances in one direction. Make two strips and sew them to opposite sides of the Star block. Press the seam allowances toward the squares. Sew six assorted 2½" squares together in the same manner. Make two strips and attach them to the remaining sides of the block. Press toward the squares.

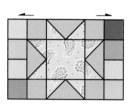 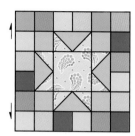

4. Make 12 flying-geese units as in step 1 using the 12 matching 2½" x 4½" rectangles for the chevron ring, and 24 light-print 2½" squares. Press the seam allowances as shown.

Make 12.

5. Repeat step 4, but this time use 12 light-print 2½" x 4½" rectangles and 24 matching print 2½" squares and press in the opposite direction. Make 12 flying-geese units. Sew each unit to a flying-geese unit from step 4 as shown. Make 12 units. Press the seam allowances open.

Make 12.

6. Sew three units from step 5 together as shown. Press the seam allowances open. Make four.

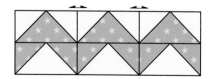

Make 4.

7. Sew a light-print 2½" square to a 2½" square of the chevron fabric used in step 6; make four. Press

the seam allowances toward the darker fabric. Sew a light-print 2½" x 4½" rectangle to the joined squares. Make two units and two mirror-image units for the block corners as shown.

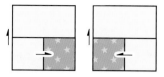

Make 2 of each.

8. Sew the corner units to opposite sides of two chevron units from step 6. Press.

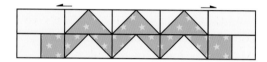

9. Sew two chevron units from step 6 to opposite sides of the block. Press the seam allowances toward the block center. Sew the chevron units from step 8 to the top and bottom of the block. Press the seam allowances toward the block center. The block should now measure 20½" x 20½".

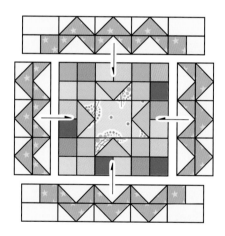

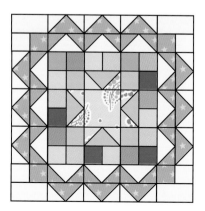

10. Repeat steps 1–9 to make a total of four blocks.

ASSEMBLING THE QUILT TOP

1. Lay out the blocks in two rows of two blocks each. When you're happy with the arrangement, sew the blocks in each row together, pinning at each of the points and seam intersections between blocks. Press the seam allowances open.
2. Sew the rows together and press the seam allowances open. The quilt center should now measure 40½" x 40½".

ADDING BORDERS AND FINISHING THE QUILT

Refer to the quilt assembly diagram at right as you add the borders. If you need more information on adding borders or finishing, visit ShopMartingale.com/HowtoQuilt.

1. Cut two light-print 2½" x 42" border strips to 40½" long. Sew the strips to the left and right sides of the quilt; press the seam allowances toward the borders.
2. Sew three light-print 2½" x 42" strips together end to end. Press the seam allowances open. Cut the long strip in half to make two border strips and trim each to 44½" long. Sew the strips to the top and bottom of the quilt; press the seam allowances toward the borders. The quilt should now measure 44½" square.
3. Draw a diagonal line from corner to corner on the wrong side of 88 light-print 2½" squares.
4. Place a marked square on the corner of an assorted 4½" square. Sew on the line and trim the seam allowances to ¼". Press the triangle toward the corner. Repeat with a second marked square on an adjacent corner of the square, orienting the diagonal in the opposite direction. Stitch, trim, and press the seam allowances toward the square. Pressing in this way makes it easier to sew the units together because the seams will oppose each other. Make 44 units.

Make 44.

5. Sew 11 units together side by side and press the seam allowances in one direction. Make four border units. Sew a 4½" square to each end of two of the border units. Press the seam allowances toward the squares.

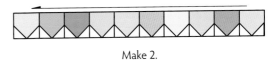

Make 2.

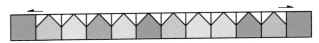

Make 2.

6. Sew the shorter border units to the left and right sides of the quilt; press the seam allowances toward the inner border. Sew border units with corner squares to the top and bottom of the quilt; press the seam allowances toward the inner border. The quilt should now measure 52½" x 52½".
7. Piece the quilt backing and prepare the binding. Layer and baste the backing, batting, and quilt top. Quilt as desired and bind your quilt.

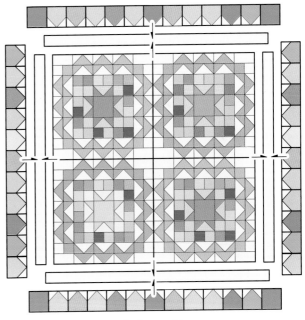

Quilt assembly

This coordinated version uses the whimsical Late Bloomers fabric by Sandy Gervais for Moda. The color palette was just my style, so I purchased a fat-quarter pack of the entire fabric line. I added some yardage for sashing, borders, backing, and binding. It was quilted using a Baptist Fan design that reinforces a traditional look.

Pieced by Nancy Allen; machine quilted by Sue Baddley with a digitized design
Finished quilt: 58½" x 80½" • **Finished block:** 20" x 20"

Most of my scraps are tone-on-tone, muted fabrics. However, I've been gradually adding brighter colors to my stash (and quilting repertoire). So while you might think this is a planned or coordinated scrap quilt, it is actually a make-do quilt. I only had to purchase fabric for the borders and backing—everything else came from my growing stash and scraps of happy-colored fabrics. Perhaps your scrap collection is made up of colors like this quilt, rather than the tone-on-tone fabrics that make up the bulk of mine. No matter what the fabric style, jump in and put those scraps to good use.

Pieced by Nancy Allen; custom machine quilted by Jen Alexander
Finished quilt: 74½" x 74½" • **Finished block:** 20" x 20"

Cherish Is the Word

Pieced by Nancy Allen; custom machine quilted by Valerie Gines
Finished quilt: 48½" x 60½" • Finished block: 12" x 12"

I used to shy away from appliquéd quilts. Although I enjoyed hand appliqué work, the process simply took longer to complete than machine piecing. When I discovered that I could machine appliqué with nearly identical results to needle-turn appliqué, I began incorporating appliqué into more of my quilts. The three quilts using this design incorporate appliqué in successively more complex blocks. The planned version is the easiest—the simple shape is appliquéd to a background fabric. The make-do version has a simple pieced background that contrasts with the appliqué pieces, and the coordinated version breaks up the block into more pieced elements with small appliquéd arcs.

The Planned Quilt

I've wanted to make a quilt of primarily polka-dot fabrics for some time. The dark-background dotted fabric really shows off the curved appliqué design. Every season you'll be able to find polka dots, but they may vary in size and color from one year to the next. I was able to combine a small white polka dot on various colors, with larger colored polka dots on bright colors, for a variety of polka-dot styles.

MATERIALS

Yardage is based on 42"-wide fabric unless otherwise noted.

1 fat eighth *each* of 12 polka-dot prints for blocks
1 fat eighth *each* of 12 coordinating solids for blocks
2⅛ yards of multicolored small-scale polka-dot print for block backgrounds
½ yard of multicolored medium-scale polka-dot print for inner border
1⅝ yards of floral for outer border*
½ yard of fabric for binding
3¼ yards of fabric for backing
57" x 69" piece of batting

*If you cut border strips crosswise and piece them, rather than cut from lengthwise strips, ⅞ yard is enough.

CUTTING

From *each* of the 12 polka-dot prints and solids, cut:
2 squares, 6½" x 6½" (48 total)

From the multicolored small-scale polka-dot print, cut:
8 strips, 7" x 42"; crosscut into 48 squares, 7" x 7"

From the multicolored medium-scale polka-dot print, cut:
5 strips, 2½" x 42"

From the floral print, cut on the *lengthwise* grain:
4 strips, 4½" x 58"

From the binding fabric, cut:
6 strips, 2¼" x 42"

MAKING THE BLOCKS

1. Draw a diagonal line from corner to corner on the wrong side of each polka-dot 6½" square.
2. Pair a marked polka-dot square with a coordinating-solid 6½" square, and place them right sides together. Sew a scant ¼" from each side of the drawn line and carefully cut on the line. Press the seam allowances toward the solid fabric. Repeat with the other two squares in the same fabric combination. You'll have four half-square-triangle units.

Make 4.

3. Using your preferred appliqué method, the appliqué pattern on page 63, and the half-square-triangle units, prepare the appliqués. (I used a freezer-paper method described on page 25.) Make sure that the fabrics are all positioned the same.

4. Align the corner of the appliqué piece with the corner of a multicolored small-scale polka-dot 7" square, pin or baste in place, and appliqué the curved edge to the background. I appliquéd by machine with monofilament and a blind hem stitch, but you can appliqué by hand if you prefer. Repeat until you've completed all four pieces for one block. Trim the finished pieces to 6½" square. The background squares were cut slightly oversize since the appliqué process can "shrink up" the background.

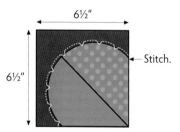

5. Carefully trim the background fabric away underneath the appliqués, leaving a ¼" seam allowance along the curved edges.

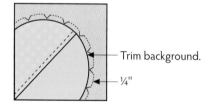

6. Lay out the four pieces of the block as shown. Sew the squares in each row together; press the seam allowances open. Then sew the two rows together and press the seam allowances open.

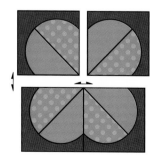 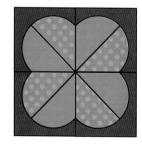

7. Repeat steps 2–6 to make a total of 12 blocks. The blocks should measure 12½" x 12½".

ASSEMBLING THE QUILT TOP

Lay out the blocks in four rows of three blocks each, as shown in the quilt assembly diagram. Sew the blocks into rows and press the seam allowances in opposite directions from row to row. Then sew the rows together and press the seam allowances in one direction. The quilt center should now measure 36½" x 48½".

ADDING BORDERS AND FINISHING THE QUILT

Measure your quilt through the center before trimming border strips to the lengths specified. Refer to the quilt assembly diagram below as you add the borders. If you need more information on adding borders or finishing, visit ShopMartingale.com/HowtoQuilt.

1. Sew three multicolored medium-scale polka-dot 2½" x 42" strips together end to end. Press the seam allowances open. Trim the strip to two 48½"-long strips, and sew the strips to opposite sides of the quilt; press the seam allowances toward the borders.

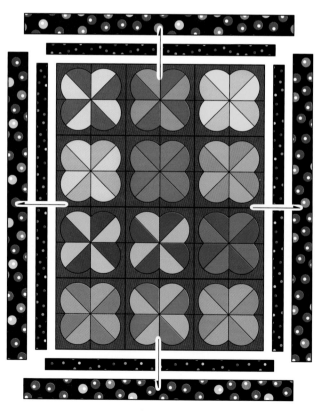

Quilt assembly

2. Trim two multicolored medium-scale polka-dot 2½" x 42" strips to 40½" long. Sew these borders to the top and bottom of the quilt top. Press the seam allowances toward the borders. The quilt should now measure 40½" x 52½".

3. Trim two lengthwise floral strips to 52½" long and two to 48½" long. Sew the 52½"-long strips to the left and right sides of the quilt center, and the 48½"-long strips to the top and bottom. Press the seam allowances toward the outer borders.

4. Piece the quilt backing and prepare the binding. Layer and baste the backing, batting, and quilt top. Quilt as desired and bind your quilt.

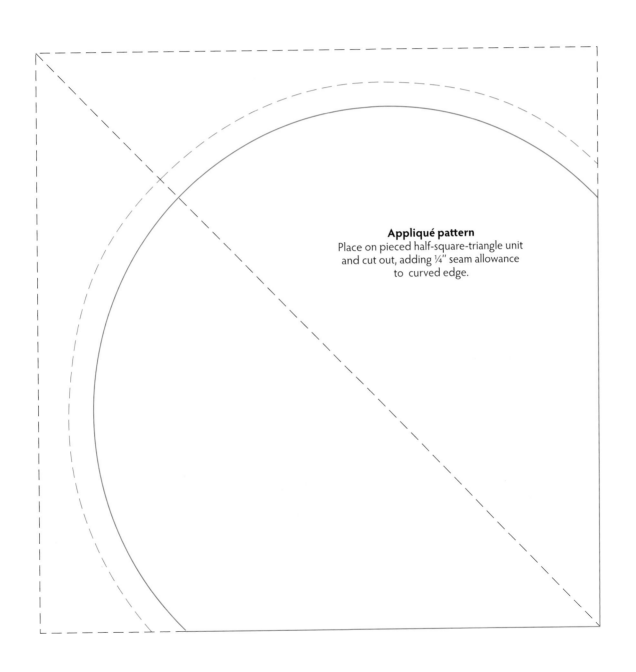

Appliqué pattern
Place on pieced half-square-triangle unit and cut out, adding ¼" seam allowance to curved edge.

What scrap quilt book would be complete without a quilt using 1930s reproduction fabrics? My earliest quilt memories are of scrap quilts my maternal grandmother made using fabrics from the 1930s, 1940s, and 1950s. I've made several quilts using 1930s reproduction fabrics, and they all remind me of her quilts, not to mention her aprons made from the same fabrics. Even today my mom can look at the Double Wedding Ring quilt made by her mother in 1952 as a wedding gift and pick out fabrics from clothes she wore as a girl, as well as those from her mother's aprons. (I'm blessed to be the protector of this family heirloom.)

The main changes to the planned version include appliquéing the blocks to a contrasting half-square-triangle background; adding a pieced border of 2" squares (that finish 1½"); and making a scalloped border, which echoes the curves in the blocks. Of course, there are also only nine blocks. I think this would be a sweet baby quilt.

Pieced by Nancy Allen; custom machine quilted by Jen Alexander
Finished quilt: 51½" x 51½" • **Finished block:** 12" x 12"

This was my first quilt using Amy Butler's wonderful fabrics. These are from her Soul Blossoms and Lotus collections. Although I wanted to have a blended look in this quilt, I added some coordinated solids so the pinwheel design in the center of each block would show up. The neutral gray sashing unifies the quilt without standing out as much as a white or a color would—not to mention that it separates the blocks so they don't blend into each other. The blocks are still the starring players of the quilt. It was quilted with variegated thread to reinforce the whimsical nature of the fabrics.

*Arcs appliquéd to Hourglass blocks
create a pinwheel design in the center.*

Pieced by Nancy Allen; machine quilted by Sue Baddley with a digitized design
Finished quilt: 67" x 67" • **Finished block:** 12" x 12"

Bull's Eye

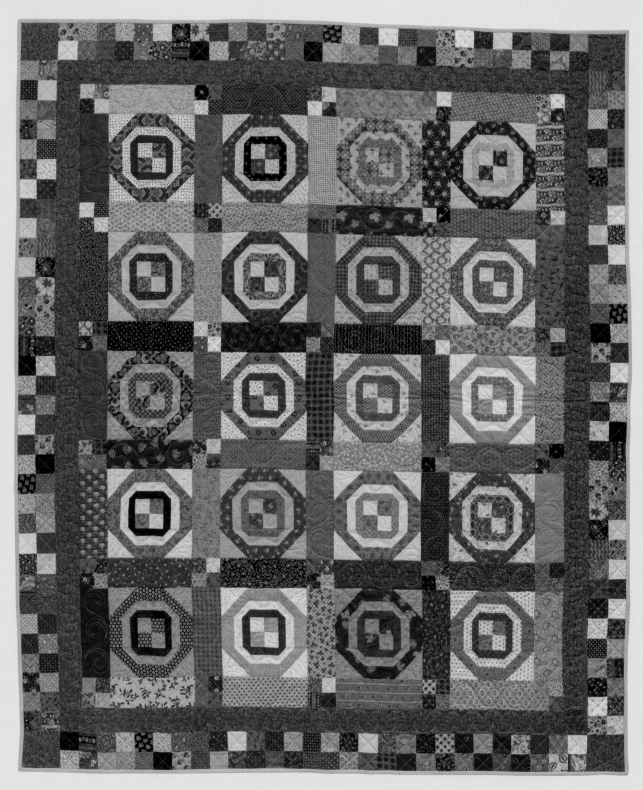

Pieced by Nancy Allen; custom machine quilted by Valerie Gines
Finished quilt: 64½" x 76½" • Finished block: 9" x 9"

 *I'm always looking for quilt patterns that have a masculine feel to them. That quest was the inspiration for this design. I found that this block goes together best if you foundation piece everything except the center four-patch unit (replaced with an hourglass unit in the coordinated version on page 71). The cutting dimensions would otherwise be down to 1/16" increments, which is hard to cut accurately and consistently. After foundation piecing the units, I trimmed them to size, removed the foundation paper, and assembled the block traditionally.*

The Make-Do Quilt

This is the perfect quilt for using up orphan two-patch and four-patch units, not to mention miscellaneous scraps as small as 2" square. The four-patch block center is echoed in the sashing cornerstones and the border. Each block uses three unique fabrics not found in any other blocks of the quilt—although they sometimes do appear in the sashing, sashing four-patch cornerstones, and checkerboard border.

MATERIALS

Yardage is based on 42"-wide fabric unless otherwise noted.

4½ yards *total* of assorted medium and dark scraps for blocks, sashing, four-patch cornerstones, and checkerboard border

2⅝ yards *total* of various light fabrics for block backgrounds, sashing, four-patch cornerstones, and checkerboard border

⅞ yard of brown print for inner border and corner squares

⅔ yard of fabric for binding

4¾ yards of fabric for backing

73" x 85" piece of batting

Foundation paper for paper piecing

Scrap Sizes

While this quilt lets you make use of some small scraps, it also calls for some chunkier pieces. You'll need two medium or dark fabrics, one piece approximately 5" x 10" and one 8" x 20" for each block. You'll also need a light background piece approximately 5" x 28" or 10" x 14".

CUTTING

From the medium and dark scraps, cut:
60 squares, 2" x 2"
124 squares, 2½" x 2½"
49 rectangles, 3½" x 9½"

From 1 medium or dark scrap, cut *for each block:*
Piece A4: 2 squares, 2" x 2"; cut each square in half diagonally to yield 4 triangles (80 total)*
Piece B1: 4 rectangles, 1¾" x 4" (80 total)*

From a second medium or dark scrap, cut *for each block:*
Piece A2: 4 rectangles, 2" x 6" (80 total)*
Piece B3: 4 rectangles, 2½" x 4" (80 total)*
2 squares, 2" x 2" (40 total)

From the light fabrics, cut:
60 squares, 2" x 2"
124 squares, 2½" x 2½"

From 1 light fabric, cut *for each block:*
Piece A1: 2 squares, 4½" x 4½"; cut each square in half diagonally to yield 4 triangles (80 total)*
Piece A3: 4 rectangles, 1½" x 4" (80 total)*
Piece B2: 4 rectangles, 2" x 4" (80 total)*
2 squares, 2" x 2" (40 total)

From the brown print, cut:
6 strips, 3" x 42"
4 squares, 4½" x 4½"

From the binding fabric, cut:
8 strips, 2¼" x 42"

*These pieces are for foundation piecing and do not have to be cut as precisely as for traditional piecing.

MAKING THE BLOCKS

1. Make 80 copies each of foundation patterns A and B on page 72.

2. Using pieces A1–A4, foundation piece pattern A. Begin with light background piece A1. Place it right side up on the unmarked side of pattern A, covering the space numbered 1 and extending ¼" beyond the diagonal line. Hold the pattern up to the light to make sure that the space is covered. Place a medium or dark A2 piece on top of piece A1, right sides together and ensuring the raw edges are aligned with the diagonal of piece A1, and pin in place. Turn the piece over and sew on the marked line. Trim the seam allowances to ¼" and press toward piece A2. Add pieces A3 and A4 in the same manner. Trim the finished unit to size and remove the paper. Make four units. For more information on foundation piecing, visit ShopMartingale.com/HowtoQuilt.

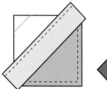

Make 4.

3. Using pieces B1–B3, foundation piece pattern B, beginning with a medium or dark piece B1 and a light background piece B2. Press the seam allowances toward the piece just added. Trim the finished unit to size and remove the paper. Make four units.

Make 4.

4. Make a four-patch unit using two light 2" squares and two medium or dark 2" squares. Spin the seam allowances as shown on page 16.

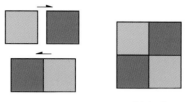

Make 1.

5. Lay out the units for the block as shown and sew them into rows; press the seam allowances as shown. Sew the rows together and press the seam allowances open.

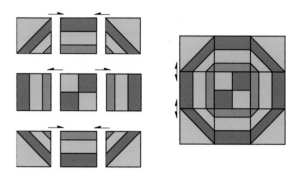

6. Repeat steps 2–5 to make a total of 20 blocks.

ASSEMBLING THE QUILT TOP

1. Lay out the blocks in five rows of four blocks each. When you're happy with the arrangement, add five 3½" x 9½" sashing rectangles to each row. Sew the blocks and sashing rectangles together. Press all seam allowances toward the sashing rectangles.

Make 5 rows.

2. Mix and match the 60 medium and dark and 60 light 2" squares into sets of four until you have 30 sets. Sew into four-patch units and spin the seam allowances. Make 30 four-patch units.

3. Sew five four-patch units from step 2 together with four 3½" x 9½" sashing rectangles as shown to make a sashing row. Press all seam allowances toward the sashing rectangles. Repeat to make six sashing rows.

Make 6.

4. Join the sashing rows and block rows, referring to the quilt assembly diagram at right. Press the seam allowances toward the sashing rows. The quilt center should now measure 38½" x 62½".

ADDING BORDERS AND FINISHING THE QUILT

Refer to the quilt assembly diagram as you add the borders. If you need more information on adding borders or finishing, visit ShopMartingale.com/HowtoQuilt.

1. Sew six brown-print 3" x 42" strips together end to end and press the seam allowances open. Cut two strips 63½" long and two strips 56½" long.

2. Sew the longer border strips to the sides of the quilt; press the seam allowances toward the borders. Sew the shorter border strips to the top and bottom of the quilt. Press the seam allowances toward the borders. The quilt should now measure 56½" x 68½".

3. Mix and match the 248 assorted light, medium, and dark 2½" squares and sew them into two-patch units; press the seam allowances toward the darker fabric. Sew 34 two-patch units together to make a side border strip. Press all seam allowances in the same direction. Make two border strips and sew them to the left and right sides of the quilt center. Press the seam allowances toward the brown-print border.

Make 2.

4. Sew 28 two-patch units together to make a top or bottom border strip; press all seam allowances in the same direction. Make two. Add a brown-print 4½" square to each end of both border strips. Press the seam allowances toward the square and sew the strips to the top and bottom of the quilt center. Press the seam allowances toward the brown-print border. Stay stitch around the outside of your quilt, about ⅛" in from the edge. The quilt center should now measure 64½" x 76½".

Make 2.

5. Piece the quilt backing and prepare the binding. Layer and baste the backing, batting, and quilt top. Quilt as desired and bind your quilt.

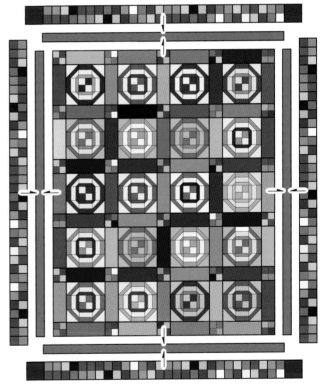

Quilt assembly

The planned version of "Bull's Eye" would be a great option to feature the team colors of your favorite college or professional athletic team. My apologies to all of the University of Michigan fans in my family for my use of Ohio State's scarlet-and-gray color palette for this quilt. It was completely unintentional! The sashing finishes at 1½" wide, and the border finishes at 3" wide.

Pieced by Nancy Allen; machine quilted by Sue Baddley with a digitized design

Finished quilt: 50" x 50" • **Finished block:** 9" x 9"

I love flannel quilts. When I rediscovered quilting in the mid-'90s, my first quilt was a flannel log cabin. The coordinated version of "Bull's Eye" uses Maywood Studio's Woolies flannels and Moda's Wool and Needle flannels. Although I used two fabric lines, they coordinate perfectly.

Rather than use a four-patch center for the block, I chose an hourglass unit. By the placement of the black and cream corner triangles in the same spot in each block, the blocks combine to create an hourglass design where they intersect. I felt this quilt did not need a border. It will be a perfect picnic or car quilt.

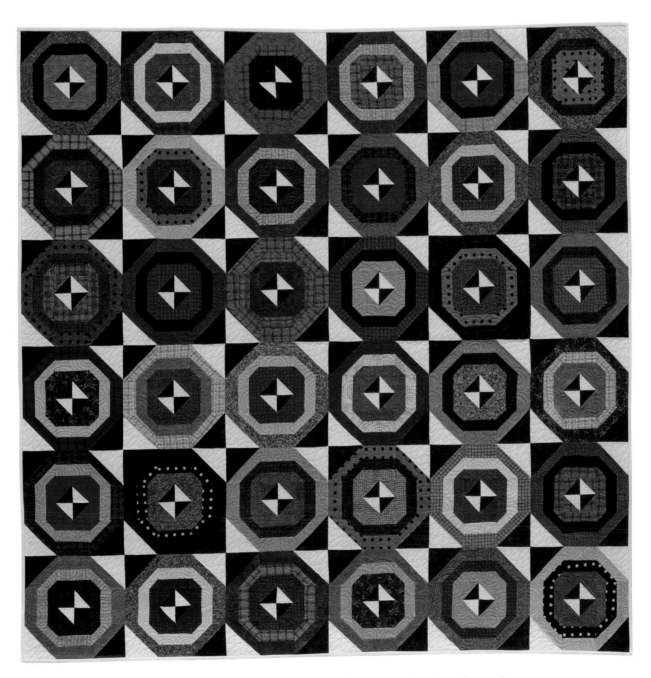

Pieced by Nancy Allen; custom machine quilted by Jen Alexander
Finished quilt: 72½" x 72½" • Finished block: 12" x 12"

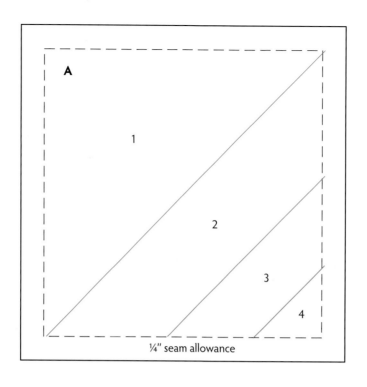

A

1

2

3

4

¼" seam allowance

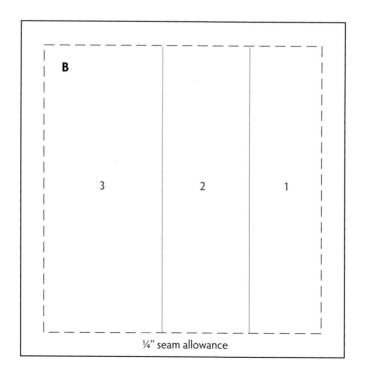

B

3

2

1

¼" seam allowance

Plaid and Pinwheels

Pieced by Nancy Allen; machine quilted by Sue Baddley with a digitized design

Finished quilt: 60½" x 84½" • **Finished block:** 10" x 10"

The blocks in the center of this quilt are very quick to sew and reminded me of a plaid—hence the name of the quilt. In fact, the blocks in the Pinwheel border will likely take longer to make than the rest of the quilt. If you need to get it done quickly, however, use the border option from the make-do version on page 79. You'll still need to make some pinwheels, but they're bigger, and you only need enough for two opposite corners of the quilt.

The Coordinated Quilt

I love all things Americana, especially the red, white, and blue fabrics by Minick and Simpson. Their American Banner Rose line—two packages of precut strips plus some yardage for borders, sashing, backing, and binding—is the perfect option for this simple project. There's no need to cut the strips for the blocks and checkerboard border if you use precuts. I used triangle paper foundations to make the half-square-triangle units for the pinwheels, but you can use whatever method you prefer.

MATERIALS

Yardage is based on 42"-wide fabric unless otherwise noted.

2 packages of precut strips (80 strips, 2½" x 42") for blocks, Pinwheel border, and checkerboard border
1 yard of beige-and-blue print for sashing
⅔ yard of navy-blue print for sashing cornerstones and first border
⅝ yard of red print for third border
⅔ yard of fabric for binding
5¼ yards of fabric for backing
69" x 93" piece of batting
Optional: 1 package of 1½" triangle paper foundations

Binding Options

I used the scraps from the backing fabric for my binding. After trimming selvages and sewing two lengths of backing fabric together, I cut the remaining length into binding strips. You could also piece the leftover precut strips into a pieced binding. Note that the binding will be 2½" wide rather than 2¼".

CUTTING

From *each* precut 2½" x 42" strip, cut:
2 strips, 2½" x 21"* (160 total)

From the beige-and-blue print, cut:
10 strips, 2½" x 42"; crosscut into 38 rectangles, 2½" x 10½"

From the navy-blue print, cut:
8 strips, 2½" x 42"; crosscut 2 of the strips into 24 squares, 2½" x 2½"

From the red print, cut:
7 strips, 2½" x 42"

From the binding fabric, cut:
8 strips, 2¼" x 42"

*Remove the selvages.

ORGANIZING YOUR FABRICS

Each block uses three different fabrics: two for the four-patch units (fabrics A and B) and one for the rectangles (fabric C).

1. Mix and match 30 coordinated half strips into pairs until you have 15 pleasing fabric combinations for the four-patch units. Identify one fabric from each pair as fabric A and the other as fabric B. Select another half strip of each fabric A and cut a 2½" square from it for the block center square.

2. From the remaining strips, including the slightly shorter fabric A strips, select 15 strips that will become the rectangles in each block, fabric C. Pair these with the 15 combinations from step 1. Crosscut each fabric C strip into 4 rectangles, 2½" x 4½".

3. Reserve the remaining strips for the Pinwheel and checkerboard borders.

MAKING THE BLOCKS

1. Sew an A strip to a B strip along the length of the strips. Press the seam allowances toward the darker fabric. Crosscut the strip set into eight segments, 2½" wide.

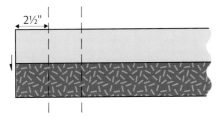

Cut 8 segments.

2. Join the two-patch units to make four-patch units with contrasting fabrics next to each other. Press the seam allowances to one side or spin the seam allowances as described in "Spinning the Seam Allowances" on page 16.

Make 4.

3. Lay out the four-patch units, one 2½" square, and the four 2½" x 4½" rectangles for one block as shown. Sew the units into rows. Press all seam allowances toward the rectangles. Join the rows to complete the block. The block should now measure 10½" x 10½".

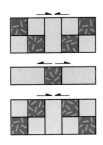 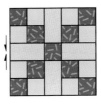

4. Repeat steps 1–3 to make a total of 15 blocks.

ASSEMBLING THE QUILT TOP

1. Lay out the blocks in five rows of three blocks each. When you're happy with the arrangement, add four beige-and-blue 2½" x 10½" sashing rectangles to the rows, alternating them with the blocks. Sew the blocks and sashing strips together in each row. Press the seam allowances toward the sashing.

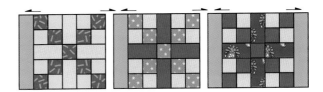

Make 5 rows.

2. Sew four navy-blue print 2½" squares and three beige-and-blue 2½" x 10½" sashing rectangles together to make a sashing row. Press the seam allowances toward the sashing rectangles. Make six rows.

Make 6.

3. Sew the six sashing rows together with the five block rows. Press the seam allowances toward the sashing rows. The quilt center should now measure 38½" x 62½".

ADDING BORDERS AND FINISHING THE QUILT

Refer to the quilt assembly diagram on page 77 as you add the borders. If you need more information on adding borders or finishing, visit ShopMartingale.com/HowtoQuilt.

First Border

1. Sew six navy-blue print 2½" x 42" strips together end to end. Press the seam allowances open. Cut two strips 62½" long and two strips 42½" long.
2. Sew the longer strips to opposite sides of the quilt. Press the seam allowances toward the borders. Sew the shorter strips to the top and bottom of the quilt and press the seam allowances toward the borders. The quilt should now measure 42½" x 66½".

Second Border

1. Select 52 of the 2½" x 21" half strips and sort them into 26 pairs. Layer the strips right sides together and cut each pair into six layered 2½" squares. Draw a diagonal line from corner to corner on the wrong side of the lighter squares, keeping the squares aligned. Sew ¼" from the drawn line on both sides and cut on the drawn line. Press the seam allowances toward the darker fabric. Make 76 sets of four matching half-square-triangle units (304 total). Trim and square up the units to measure 2" square. I was able to get 12 half-square-triangle units from each pair of strips—enough for three Pinwheel blocks.

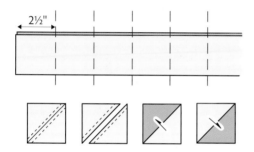

2. Join four matching half-square-triangle units as shown to make a Pinwheel block that measures 3½" square. I suggest you "spin the seam allowances" so the seams will oppose each other when you sew the Pinwheel blocks together. Make a total of 76 blocks.

Make 76.

3. Sew 22 Pinwheel blocks together side by side. Make two of these border strips and sew them to opposite sides of the quilt. Join 16 Pinwheel blocks together in the same manner; make two. Sew these border strips to the top and bottom of the quilt. Press all seam allowances toward the navy-blue borders. The quilt should now measure 48½" x 72½".

Make 2 rows with 16 pinwheels.
Make 2 rows with 22 pinwheels.

Third Border

1. Sew seven red-print 2½" x 42" strips together end to end. Press the seam allowances open and cut two strips 72½" long and two strips 52½" long.

2. Sew the longer borders to the left and right sides of the quilt; press the seam allowances toward the red borders. Sew the shorter borders to the top and bottom of the quilt and press the seam allowances toward the red borders. The quilt should now measure 52½" x 76½".

Fourth Border

1. Select 40 of the 2½" x 21" strips and sort them into 20 pairs. Sew each pair of strips together to make a strip set. Press the seam allowances toward the darker fabric. Crosscut the strip sets into 2½"-wide segments until you have a total of 136 two-patch units.

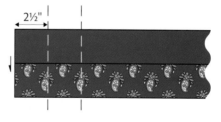

Make 20 strip sets.
Cut 136 segments.

2. Mix and match two-patch units and sew them into two borders with 38 two-patch units each and two borders with 30 two-patch units each. Alternate the direction of the light and dark fabrics so that the seam allowances will oppose each other and to enhance the checkerboard design.

Make 2 rows with 38 units.

Make 2 rows with 30 units.

3. Attach the longer border strips to the left and right sides of the quilt, and the shorter border strips to the top and bottom of the quilt. Press the seam allowances toward the red borders. The quilt should now measure 60½" x 84½". Stay stitch around the outside of your quilt, about ⅛" in from the edge.

4. Piece the quilt backing and prepare the binding. Layer and baste the backing, batting, and quilt top. Quilt as desired and bind your quilt.

Quilt assembly

I love the sophistication of this pink-and-gray color palette. I kept the blocks and sashing fairly subtle by using only medium and light fabrics, and I brought darker fabrics into the pieced borders to frame the quilt center.

This quilt lends itself to many other planned color schemes or fabric collections: Christmas prints, Civil War browns and blues, spring pastels, or even a variety of florals for a blended look. Like the coordinated version (page 73), this quilt is make from 2½"-wide strips.

Pieced by Nancy Allen; custom machine quilted by Catherine Timmons
Finished quilt: 72½" x 72½" • **Finished block:** 10" x 10"

I emphasized the geometric style of this quilt by piecing the sashing border with 2½" squares (that finish at 2") and adding the bold black 3"-wide borders (cut the strips 3½" wide). Although you could skip making the pinwheels entirely and use a single-fabric border instead of the pinwheel border, this variation has only 26 pinwheels that finish at 4". The outer border is pieced from 4" squares that finish at 3½".

Pieced by Nancy Allen; machine quilted by Sue Baddley with a digitized design
Finished quilt: 77½" x 77½" • Finished block: 10" x 10"

About the Author

Having grown up surrounded by quilts made by both of her grandmothers, Nancy Allen started her first quilt when she was about 12 years old. It was an appliquéd and embroidered flower-girl quilt using scraps from her mother and grandmother. Her mother ended up finishing the quilt because Nancy quickly lost interest.

About 10 years later, she sewed Double Irish Chain quilt tops from 2" squares for a woman in her neighborhood. The quilts were then quilted by hand and sold at a boutique in Salt Lake City, Utah. How much easier this would have been with strip-piecing techniques, but this was before rotary cutters. Subsequent years found Nancy focused on decorative painting and counted cross-stitch as she pursued a career in high-tech software marketing.

In 1995, when she lived near Amish country in Lancaster County, Pennsylvania, she rediscovered quiltmaking and dusted off her sewing machine. Most of her other hobbies have been pushed aside as she's made more than 100 quilts—with even more quilt tops waiting to be quilted. By her estimate, Nancy has a big enough stash of blocks of the month, quilt kits, and fabric that she could make more than 50 quilts without buying fabric except perhaps for backing. This book was a first step at digging into that stash. She hopes that these quilts inspire quilters to use up some fabric—or perhaps to buy some more.

Keep up with what Nancy is working on at BountifulHeirlooms.blogspot.com.